Cloud Native

Using Containers, Functions, and Data to Build
Next-Generation Applications

Boris Scholl, Trent Swanson, and Peter Jausovec

Beijing · Boston · Farnham · Sebastopol · Tokyo

Cloud Native

by Boris Scholl, Trent Swanson, and Peter Jausovec

Published by O'Reilly Media, Inc., 1005 Gravenstein Highway North, Sebastopol, CA 95472.

O'Reilly books may be purchased for educational, business, or sales promotional use. Online editions are also available for most titles (*http://oreilly.com*). For more information, contact our corporate/institutional sales department: 800-998-9938 or *corporate@oreilly.com*.

Acquisitions Editor: Kathleen Carr	**Indexer:** Ellen Troutman-Zaig
Development Editor: Nicole Tache	**Interior Designer:** David Futato
Production Editor: Elizabeth Kelly	**Cover Designer:** Karen Montgomery
Copyeditor: Octal Publishing, Inc.	**Illustrator:** Rebecca Demarest
Proofreader: Rachel Monaghan	

September 2019:   First Edition

Revision History for the First Edition

2019-08-21:   First Release
2019-12-10:   Second Release
2020-02-07:   Third Release

See *http://oreilly.com/catalog/errata.csp?isbn=9781492053828* for release details.

978-1-492-05382-8

[LSI]

Table of Contents

Preface

Thought leaders across different companies and industries have been restating Watts Humphrey's statement, "Every business will become a software business." He was spot on. Software is taking over the world and is challenging the status quo of existing companies. Netflix has revolutionized how we obtain and consume TV and movies, Uber has transformed the transportation industry, and Airbnb is challenging the hotel industry. A couple of years ago that would have been unthinkable, but software has allowed new companies to venture into all industries and establish new thinking and business models.

The previously mentioned companies are often referred to as "born-in-the-cloud companies," which means that at the basis of their offerings are services running in the cloud. Those services are built in a way that companies can quickly react to market and customer demands, release updates and fixes in a short period of time, use the latest technologies, and take advantage of the improved economics provided by the cloud. Services built in a cloud native way have also allowed companies to rethink their business models and move to new ones, such as subscription-based models. Such services are often referred to as *cloud native applications*.

The success and popularity of cloud native applications have led many enterprises to adopt cloud native architectures, even bringing many of the concepts to on-premises applications.

At the heart of cloud native applications are *containers, functions,* and *data*. There are many books out there focusing on each of these specific technologies. Cloud native applications use all of these technologies and take advantage of and exploit all of the benefits of the cloud. We, the authors, have seen many customers struggle to piece all of those technologies together to design and develop cloud native applications, so we decided to write a book with the goal to provide the foundational knowledge that enables developers and architects alike to get started with designing cloud native applications.

This book starts by laying down the foundation for the reader to understand the basic principles of distributed computing and how they relate to cloud native applications, as well as providing a closer look at containers and functions. Further, it covers service communication patterns, resiliency, and data patterns as well as providing guidance on when to use what. The book concludes by explaining the DevOps approach, portability considerations, and a collection of best practices that we have seen to be useful in successful cloud native applications.

The book is not a step-by-step implementation guide for building cloud native applications for a specific set of requirements. After reading this book, you should have the understanding and knowledge to help design, build, and operate successful cloud native applications. Tutorials are great for working through very specific needs, but a fundamental understanding of building cloud native applications provides teams with the necessary skills to ship successful cloud native applications.

Conventions Used in This Book

The following typographical conventions are used in this book:

Italic
> Indicates new terms, URLs, email addresses, filenames, and file extensions.

`Constant width`
> Used for program listings, as well as within paragraphs to refer to program elements such as variable or function names, databases, data types, environment variables, statements, and keywords.

`Constant width bold`
> Shows commands or other text that should be typed literally by the user.

`Constant width italic`
> Shows text that should be replaced with user-supplied values or by values determined by context.

 This element signifies a tip or suggestion.

 This element signifies a general note.

This element indicates a warning or caution.

O'Reilly Online Learning

 For almost 40 years, *O'Reilly Media* has provided technology and business training, knowledge, and insight to help companies succeed.

Our unique network of experts and innovators share their knowledge and expertise through books, articles, conferences, and our online learning platform. O'Reilly's online learning platform gives you on-demand access to live training courses, in-depth learning paths, interactive coding environments, and a vast collection of text and video from O'Reilly and 200+ other publishers. For more information, please visit *http://oreilly.com*.

How to Contact Us

Please address comments and questions concerning this book to the publisher:

> O'Reilly Media, Inc.
> 1005 Gravenstein Highway North
> Sebastopol, CA 95472
> 800-998-9938 (in the United States or Canada)
> 707-829-0515 (international or local)
> 707-829-0104 (fax)

We have a web page for this book, where we list errata, examples, and any additional information. You can access this page at *http://bit.ly/cloud-native-1e*.

To comment or ask technical questions about this book, send email to *bookquestions@oreilly.com*.

For more information about our books, courses, conferences, and news, see our website at *http://www.oreilly.com*.

Find us on Facebook: *http://facebook.com/oreilly*

Follow us on Twitter: *http://twitter.com/oreillymedia*

Watch us on YouTube: *http://www.youtube.com/oreillymedia*

Acknowledgments

We would like to thank Nicole Taché, our editor at O'Reilly, as well as the tech reviewers and beta reviewers for their valuable contributions to the book. In addition, we would like to thank Haishi Bai and Bhushan Nene for their thorough reviews and suggestions to improve the quality of the book.

Boris would like to thank his wife, Christina, and his kids, Marie and Anton, for being so patient and supportive during the time he was working on the book.

Trent would like to thank his wife, Lisa, and his son, Mark, for their support and patience while he was working on this book.

Peter would like to thank his wife, Nives, for her support, encouragement, and understanding while he was working nights and weekends on this book.

CHAPTER 1

Introduction to Cloud Native

What are cloud native applications? What makes them so appealing that the cloud native model is now considered not only for the cloud, but also for the edge? And, finally, how do you design and develop cloud native applications? These are all questions that will be answered throughout this book. But before we dive into the details on the what, why, and how, we want to provide a brief introduction to the cloud native world and some of the fundamental concepts and assumptions that are building the foundation for modern cloud native applications and environments.

Distributed Systems

One of the biggest hurdles that developers face when they build cloud native applications for the first time is that they must deal with services that are not on the same machine, and they need to deal with patterns that consider a network between the machines. Without even knowing it, they have entered the world of distributed systems. A *distributed system* is a system in which individual computers are connected through a network and appear as a single computer. Being able to distribute computing power across a bunch of machines is a great way to accomplish scalability, reliability, and better economics. For example, most cloud providers are using cheaper commodity hardware and solving common problems such as high availability and reliability through software-based solutions.

Fallacies of Distributed Systems

There are couple of incorrect or unfounded assumptions most developers and architects make when they enter the world of distributed systems. Peter Deutsch, a Fellow at Sun Microsystems, was identifying fallacies of distributed computing back in 1994, at a time when nobody thought about cloud computing. Because cloud native applications are, at their core, distributed systems, these fallacies still have validity today.

Following is the list of the fallacies that Deutsch described, with their meanings applied to cloud native applications:

The network is reliable

Even in the cloud you cannot assume that the network is reliable. Because services are typically placed on different machines, you need to develop your software in a way that it accounts for potential network failures, which we discuss later in this book.

Latency is zero

Latency and bandwidth are often confused, but it is important to understand the difference. Latency is how much time goes by until data is received, whereas bandwidth indicates how much data can be transferred in a given window of time. Because latency has a big impact on user experience and performance, you should take care to do the following:

- Avoid frequent network calls and introducing chattiness to the network.

- Design your cloud native application in a way that the data is closest to your client by using caching, content delivery networks (CDNs), and multiregion deployments.

- Use publication/subscription (pub/sub) mechanisms to be notified that there is new data and store it locally to be immediately available. Chapter 3 covers messaging patterns such as pub/sub in more detail.

There is infinite bandwidth

Nowadays, network bandwidth does not seem to be a big issue, but new technologies and areas such as edge computing open up new scenarios that demand far more bandwidth. For example, it is predicted that a self-driving car will produce around 50 terabytes (TB) of data per day. This volume of data requires you to design your cloudnative application with bandwidth usage in mind. Domain-Driven Design (DDD) and data patterns such as Command Query Responsibility Segregation (CQRS) are very useful under such bandwidth-demanding circumstances. Chapter 4 and Chapter 6 cover how to work with data in cloud native applications in more detail.

The network is secure

Two things are often an afterthought for developers: diagnostics and security. The assumption that networks are secure can be fatal. As a developer or architect, you need to make security a priority of your design; for example, by embracing a defense-in-depth approach.

The topology does not change

Pets versus cattle is a meme that gained popularity with the advent of containers. It means that you do not treat any machine as a known entity (pet) with its own set of properties, such as static IPs and so on. Instead, you treat machines as a member of a herd that has no special attributes. This concept is very important with cloud native applications. Because cloud environments are meant to provide elasticity, machines can be added and removed based on criteria such as resource consumption or requests per second.

There is one administrator

In traditional software development, it was quite common to have one person responsible for the environment, installing and upgrading the application, and so forth. Modern cloud architectures and DevOps methods have shifted the way software is built. A modern cloud native application is a composite of many services that need to work together in concert and that are developed by different teams. This makes it practically impossible for a single person to know and understand the application in its entirety, not to mention trying to fix a problem. Thus, you need to ensure that you have governance in place that makes it easy to troubleshoot issues. Throughout this book, we introduce you to important concepts such as *release management*, *decoupling*, and *logging and monitoring*. Chapter 5 provides a detailed look at common DevOps practices for cloud native applications.

Transport cost is zero

From a cloud native perspective, there are two ways to look at this one. First, transport happens over a network and network costs are not free with most cloud providers. Most cloud providers, for example, do not charge for data ingress, but do charge for data egress. The second way to look at this fallacy is that the cost for translating any payload into objects is not free. For example, serialization and deserialization are usually fairly expensive operations that you need to consider in addition to the latency of network calls.

The network is homogeneous

This is almost not worth listing given that pretty much every developer and architect understands that there are different protocols that they must consider when building their applications.

As mentioned before, although these fallacies were documented a long time ago, they are still a good reminder of the incorrect assumptions people make when entering the cloud native world. Throughout this book, we teach you patterns and best practices that take all of the fallacies of distributed computing into account.

CAP Theorem

The CAP theorem is often mentioned in combination with distributed systems. The CAP theorem states that any networked shared-data system can have at most two of the following three desirable properties:

- Consistency (C) equivalent to having a single up-to-date copy of the data
- High availability (A) of that data (for updates)
- Tolerance to network partitions (P)

The reality is that you will always have network partitions (remember, "the network is reliable" is one of the fallacies of distributed computing). That leaves you with only two choices—you can optimize either for consistency or high availability. Many NoSQL databases such as Cassandra optimize for availability, whereas SQL-based systems that adhere to the principles of ACID (atomicity, consistency, isolation, and durability) optimize for consistency.

The Twelve-Factor App

In the early days of Infrastructure as a Service (IaaS) and Platform as a Service (PaaS), it quickly became obvious that the cloud required a new way of developing applications. For example, on-premises scaling was often done by scaling vertically, meaning adding more resources to a machine. Scaling in the cloud, on the other hand, is usually done horizontally, meaning adding more machines to distribute the load. This type of scaling requires stateless applications, and this is one of the factors described by the *Twelve-Factor App manifesto*. The Twelve-Factor App methodology can be considered the foundation for cloud native applications and was first introduced by engineers at Heroku, derived from best practices for application development in the cloud. Cloud development has evolved since the introduction of the Twelve-Factor manifesto, but the principles still apply. Following are the 12 factors and their meaning for cloud native applications:

1. Codebase

   One codebase tracked in revision control; many deploys.

   There is only one codebase per application, but it can be deployed into many environments such as Dev, Test, and Prod. In cloud native architecture, this translates directly into one codebase per service or function, each having its own Continuous Integration/Continuous Deployment (CI/CD) flow.

2. Dependencies

   Explicitly declare and isolate dependencies.

   Declaring and isolating dependencies is an important aspect of cloud native development. Many issues arise due to missing dependencies or version mismatch of dependencies, which stem from environmental differences between the on-premises and cloud environments. In general, you should always use dependency managers for languages such as Maven or npm. Containers have drastically reduced dependency-based issues because all dependencies are packaged inside a container, and as such should be declared in the Dockerfile. Chef, Puppet, Ansible, and Terraform are great tools to manage and install system dependencies.

3. Configuration

Store configuration in the environment.

Configuration should be strictly separated from code. This allows you to easily apply configurations per environment. For example, you can have a test configuration file that stores all the connection strings and other information used in a test environment. If you want to deploy the same application to a production environment, you need only to replace the configuration. Many modern platforms support external configuration, whether it is configuration maps with Kubernetes or managed configuration services in cloud environments.

4. Backing Services

Treat backing services as attached resources.

A backing service is defined as "any service the app consumed over the network as part of its normal operation." In the case of cloud native applications, this might be a managed caching service or a Database as a Service (DbaaS) implementation. The recommendation here is to access those services through configuration settings stored in external configuration systems, which allows loose coupling, one of the principles that is also valid for cloud native applications.

5. Build, Release, Run

Strictly separate build and run stages.

As you will see in Chapter 5 on DevOps, it is recommended to aim for fully automated build and release stages using CI/CD practices.

6. Processes

Execute the app in one or more stateless processes.

As mentioned earlier, compute in the cloud should be stateless, meaning that data should only be saved outside the processes. This enables elasticity, which is one of the promises of cloud computing.

7. Data Isolation

Each service manages its own data.

This is one of the key tenets of *microservices architectures*, which is a common pattern in cloud native applications. Each service manages its own data, which can be accessed only through APIs, meaning that other services that are part of the application are not allowed to directly access the data of another service.

8. Concurrency

Scale out via the process model.

Improved scale and resource usage are two of the key benefits of cloud native applications, meaning that you can scale each service or function independently and horizontally; thus, you'll achieve better resource usage.

9. Disposability

   Maximize robustness with fast startup and graceful shutdown.

   Containers and functions already satisfy this factor given that both provide fast startup times. One thing that is often neglected is to design for a crash or scale in scenario, meaning that the instance count of a function or a container is decreased, which is also captured in this factor.

10. Dev/Prod Parity

    Keep development, staging, and production as similar as possible.

    Containers allow you to package all of the dependencies of your service, which limits the issues with environment inconsistencies. There are scenarios that are a bit trickier, especially when you use managed services that are not available on-premises in your Dev environment. Chapter 5 looks at methods and techniques to keep your environments as consistent as possible.

11. Logs

    Treat logs as event streams.

    Logging is one of the most important tasks in a distributed system. There are so many moving parts and without a good logging strategy, you would be "flying blind" when the application is not behaving as expected. The Twelve-Factor manifesto states that you should treat logs as streams, routed to external systems.

12. Admin Processes

    Run admin and management tasks as one-off processes.

    This basically means that you should execute administrative and management tasks as short-lived processes. Both functions and containers are great tools for that.

Throughout the book you will recognize many of these factors because they are still very relevant for cloud native applications.

Availability and Service-Level Agreements

Most of the time, cloud native applications are composite applications that use compute, such as containers and functions, but also managed cloud services such as DbaaS, caching services, and/or identity services. What is not obvious is that your compound Service-Level Agreement (SLA) will never be as high as the highest availability of an individual service. SLAs are typically measured in uptime in a year, more commonly referred to as "number of nines." Table 1-1 shows a list of common availability percentages for cloud services and their corresponding downtimes.

Table 1-1. Uptime percentages and service downtime

Availability %	Downtime per year	Downtime per month	Downtime per week
99%	3.65 days	7.20 hours	1.68 hours
99.9%	8.76 hours	43.2 minutes	10.1 minutes
99.99%	52.56 minutes	4.32 minutes	1.01 minutes
99.999%	5.26 minutes	25.9 seconds	6.05 seconds
99.9999%	31.5 seconds	2.59 seconds	0.605 seconds

Following is an example of a compound SLA:

Service 1 (99.95%) + Service 2 (99.90%): $0.9995 \times 0.9990 = 0.9985005$

The compound SLA is 99.85%.

Summary

Many developers struggle when starting to develop for the cloud. In a nutshell, developers are facing three major challenges: first, they need to understand distributed systems; second, they need to understand new technologies such as containers and functions; and third, they need to understand what patterns to use when building cloud native applications. Having some familiarity with the fundamentals, such as the fallacies of distributed systems, the Twelve-Factor manifesto, and compound SLAs, will make the transition easier. This chapter introduced some of the fundamental concepts of cloud native, which enables you to better understand some of the architectural considerations and patterns discussed throughout the book.

CHAPTER 2

Fundamentals

As discussed in Chapter 1, cloud native applications are applications that are distributed in nature and utilize cloud infrastructure. There are many technologies and tools that are being used to implement cloud native applications, but from a compute perspective, it is mainly *functions* and *containers*. From an architectural perspective, *microservices architectures* have gained a lot of popularity. More often than not, those terms are mistakenly used, and often believed to be one and the same. In reality, functions and containers are different technologies, each serving a particular purpose, whereas microservices describes an architectural style. That said, understanding how to best use functions and containers, along with *eventing* or *messaging* technologies, allows developers to design, develop, and operate a new generation of cloud native microservices-based applications in the most efficient and agile way. To make the correct architectural decisions to design those types of applications, it is important to understand the basics of the underlying terms and technologies. This chapter explains important technologies used with cloud native applications and concludes by providing an overview of the microservices architectural style.

Containers

Initially, containers were brought into the spotlight by startups and born-in-the-cloud companies, but over the past couple of years, containers have become synonymous with application modernization. Today there are very few companies that are not using containers or at least considering using containers in the future, which means that architects and developers alike need to understand what containers offer and what they don't offer.

When people talk about containers today, they refer to "Docker containers" most of the time, because it's Docker that has really made containers popular. However, in the Linux operating system (OS) world, containers date back more than 10 years. The initial idea of containers was to slice up an OS so that you can securely run multiple applications without them interfering with one another. The required isolation is accomplished through namespaces and control groups, which are Linux kernel features. Namespaces allow the different components of the OS to be sliced up and thus create isolated workspaces. Control groups then allow fine-grained control of resource utilization, effectively stopping one container from consuming all system resources.

Because the interaction with kernel features was not exactly what we would call developer friendly, Linux containers (LXC) were introduced to abstract away some of the complexity of composing the various technology underpinnings of what is now commonly call a "container." Eventually it was Docker that made containers mainstream by introducing a developer-friendly packaging of the kernel features. Docker defines containers as a "standardized unit of software." The "unit of software"—or, more accurately, the service or application running within a container—has full, private access to their own isolated view of OS constructs. In other words, you can view containers as encapsulated, individually deployable components running as isolated instances on the same kernel with virtualization happening on the OS level.

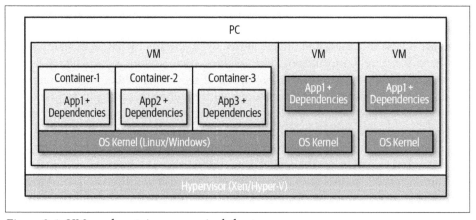

Figure 2-1. VMs and containers on a single host

In addition, containers use the copy-on-write filesystem strategy, which allows multiple containers to share the same data, and the OS provides a copy of the data to the container that needs to modify or write data. This allows containers to be very lightweight in terms of memory and disk space usage, resulting in faster startup times, which is one of the great benefits of using containers. Other benefits are *deterministic deployments*, allowing portability between environments, isolation, and higher density. For modern cloud native applications, container images have become the unit of deployment encapsulating the application or service code, its runtime, dependencies, system libraries, and so on. Due to their fast startup times, containers are an ideal technology for scale-out scenarios, which are very common in cloud native applications. Figure 2-1 shows the difference between virtual machines (VMs) and containers on a single host.

Container Isolation Levels

Because containers are based on OS virtualization, they share the same kernel when running on the same host. Although this is sufficient enough isolation for most scenarios, it falls short of the isolation level that hardware-based virtualization options such as VMs provide. Following are some of the downsides of using VMs as the foundation of cloud native applications:

- VMs can take a considerable amount of time to start because they boot a full OS.
- The size of the VM can be an issue. A VM contains an entire OS, which can easily be several gigabytes in size. Copying this image across a network—for example, if they are kept in a central image repository—will take a lot of time.
- Scaling of VMs has its challenges. Scaling up (adding more resources) requires a new, larger VM (more CPU, memory, storage, etc.) to be provisioned and booted. Scaling out might not be fast enough to respond to demand; it takes time for new instances to start.
- VMs have more overhead and use considerably more resources such as memory, CPU, and disk. This limits the density, or number of VMs that can run on a single host machine.

The most common scenarios that demand high isolation on a hardware virtualization level are hostile multitenant scenarios in which you typically need to protect against malicious escape and breakout attempts into other targets on the same host or on the shared infrastructure. Cloud providers have been using technologies internally that provide VM-level isolation while maintaining the expected speed and efficiency of containers. These technologies are known as *Hyper-V containers*, *sandboxed containers*, or *MicroVMs*. Here are the most popular MicroVM technologies (in nonspecific order):

Nabla containers (https://nabla-containers.github.io/)
These enable better isolation by taking advantage of unikernel techniques, specifically those from the Solo5 project (*https://github.com/Solo5/solo5*), to limit system calls from the container to host kernel. The Nabla container runtime (runc) is an Open Container Initiative (OCI)-compliant runtime. OCI will be explained in a bit more detail later in this chapter.

Google's gVisor (https://github.com/google/gvisor)
This is a container runtime and user space kernel written in Go. The new kernel is a "user space" process that addresses the container's system call needs,

preventing direct interaction with the host OS. The gVisor runtime (runSC) is an OCI-compliant runtime, and it supports Kubernetes orchestration as well.

Microsoft's Hyper-V containers (https://oreil.ly/5njcd)

Microsoft's Hyper-V containers were introduced a couple of years ago and are based on VM Worker Process (*vmwp.exe*). Those containers provide full VM-level isolation and are OCI compliant. As for running Hyper-V containers in Kubernetes (*http://bit.ly/33vZb7U*) in production, you will want to wait for general availability of Kubernetes on Windows.

Kata containers (https://katacontainers.io/)

Kata containers are a combination of Hyper.sh and Intel's clear containers and provide classic hardware-assisted virtualization. Kata containers are compatible with the OCI specification for Docker containers and CRI for Kubernetes.

Amazon's Firecracker

Firecracker is powering Amazon's Lambda infrastructure and has been open sourced under the Apache 2.0 license. Firecracker is a user-mode VM solution that sits on top of the KVM API and is designed to run modern Linux kernels. The goal of Firecracker is to provide support for running Linux containers in a hypervisor-isolated fashion similar to other more isolated container technologies such as Kata containers. Note that, as of this writing, you are not able to use Firecracker with Kubernetes, Docker, or Kata containers.

Figure 2-2 provides an overview of the isolation levels of the these technologies.

	VM	Kata/gVisor/ Hyper-V/Firecracker	Nabla	Container	Process
Hardware	Shared	Shared	Shared	Shared	Shared
OS Kernel	Not shared	Not shared	Shared, OS calls blocked	Shared	Shared
System Resources (ex: File System)	Not shared	Not shared	Not shared	Shared	Shared

Figure 2-2. Isolation levels for VMs, containers, and processes

Container Orchestration

To manage the life cycle of containers at scale, you need to use a container orchestrator. The tasks of a container orchestrator are the following:

- The provisioning and deployment of containers onto the cluster nodes
- Resource management of containers, meaning placing containers on nodes that provide sufficient resources or moving containers to other nodes if the resource limits of a node is reached
- Health monitoring of the containers and the nodes to initiaing restarted and rescheduling in case of failures on a container or node level
- Scaling in or out containers within a cluster
- Providing mappings for containers to connect to networking
- Internal load balancing between containers

There are multiple container orchestrators available, but there is no doubt that Kubernetes is by far the most popular choice for cluster management and the scheduling of container-centric workloads in a cluster.

Kubernetes Overview

Kubernetes (often abbreviated as k8s) is an open source project for running and managing containers. Google open sourced the project in 2014, and Kubernetes is often viewed as a container platform, microservices platform, and/or a cloud portability layer. All of the major cloud vendors have a managed Kubernetes offering today.

A Kubernetes cluster runs multiple components that can be grouped in one of three categories: *master components*, *node components*, or *addons*. Master components provide the cluster control plane. These components are responsible for making cluster-wide decisions like scheduling tasks in the cluster or responding to events, such as starting new tasks if one fails or does not meet the desired number of replicas. The master components can run on any node in the cluster, but are commonly deployed to dedicated master nodes. Managed Kubernetes offerings from cloud providers will handle the management of the control plane, including on-demand upgrades and patches.

Kubernetes master components include the following:

kube-apiserver
    Exposes the Kubernetes API and is the frontend for the Kubernetes control plane

etcd
    A key/value store used for all cluster data

kube-scheduler
> Monitors newly created *pods* (a Kubernetes-specific management wrapper around containers, which we explain in more detail later in this chapter) that are not assigned to a node and finds an available node

kube-controller-manager
> Manages a number of controllers that are responsible for responding to nodes that go down or maintaining the correct number of replicas

cloud-controller-manager
> Run controllers that interact with the underlying cloud providers

Node components run on every node in the cluster, which is also referred to as the *data plane*, and are responsible for maintaining running pods and the environment for the node to which they are deployed.

Kubernetes node components include the following:

kubelet
> An agent that runs on each node in the cluster and is responsible for running containers in pods based on their pod specification

kube-proxy
> Maintains network rules on the nodes and performs connection forwarding

container runtime
> The software responsible for running containers (see "Kubernetes and Containers" on page 16)

Figure 2-3 shows the Kubernetes master and worker node components.

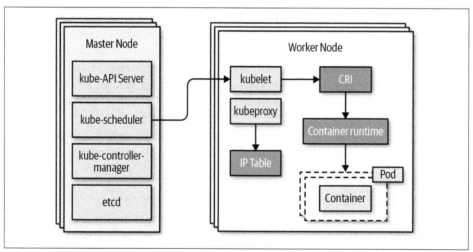

Figure 2-3. Kubernetes master and worker node components

Kubernetes is commonly deployed with addons that are managed by the master and worker node components. These addons will include services like Domain Name System (DNS) and a management user interface (UI).

A deep dive into Kubernetes is beyond the scope of this book. There are, however, some fundamental concepts that are important for you to understand:

Pods
> A pod is basically a management wrapper around one or multiple containers, storage resources, or a unique network IP, that governs the container life cycle. Although Kubernetes supports multiple containers per pod, most of the time there is only one application container per pod. That said, the pattern of *sidecar containers*, which extends or enhances the functionality of the application container, is very popular. Service meshes like Istio rely heavily on sidecars, as you can see in Chapter 3.

Services
> A Kubernetes service provides a steady endpoint to a grouping of pods that are running on the cluster. Kubernetes uses label selectors to identify which pods are targeted by a service.

ReplicaSets
> The easiest way to think about ReplicaSets is to think about service instances. You basically define how many replicas of a pod you need, and Kubernetes makes sure that you have that number of replicas running at any given time.

Deployments
> The Kubernetes Deployment documentation states that you "describe a desired state in a Deployment object, and the Deployment controller changes the actual state to the desired state at a controlled rate." In other words, you should use Deployments for rolling out and monitoring ReplicaSets, scaling ReplicaSets, updating pods, rolling back to earlier Deployments versions, and cleaning up older ReplicaSets.

Figure 2-4 provides a logical view of the fundamental Kubernetes concepts and how they interact with one another.

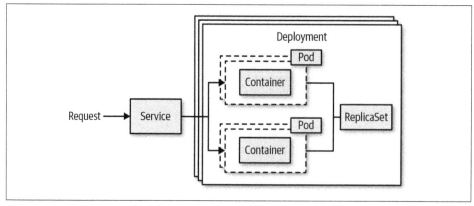

Figure 2-4. Fundamental Kubernetes concepts

Kubernetes and Containers

Kubernetes is simply the orchestration platform for containers, so it needs a container runtime to manage the container life cycle. The Docker runtime was supported from day one in Kubernetes, but it isn't the only container runtime available on the market. As a consequence, the Kubernetes community has pushed for a generic way to integrate container runtimes into Kubernetes. Interfaces have proven to be a good software pattern for providing contracts between two systems, so the community created the Container Runtime Interface (CRI) (*http://bit.ly/31y3pdC*). The CRI avoids "hardcoding" specific runtime requirements into the Kubernetes codebase, with the consequence of always needing to update the Kubernetes codebase when there are changes to a container runtime. Instead, the CRI describes the functions that need to be implemented by a container runtime to be CRI compliant. The functions that the CRI describes handle the life cycle of container pods (start, stop, pause, kill, delete), container image management (e.g., download images from a registry), and some helper functions around observability, such as log and metric collections and networking. Figure 2-5 shows high-level CRI example architectures for Docker and Kata containers.

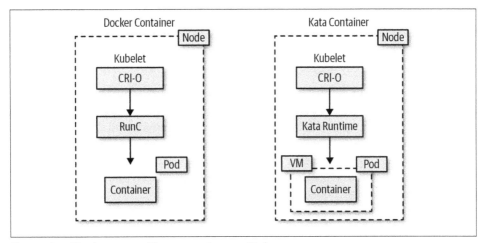

Figure 2-5. Docker versus Kata container on Kubernetes

The following list provides other container-related technologies that might be useful:

OCI
> The OCI is a Linux Foundation (*https://en.wikipedia.org/wiki/Linux_Foundation*) project that aims to design open standards for container images and runtimes. Many container technologies implement an OCI-compliant runtime and image specification.

containerd
> containerd is an industry-standard container runtime used by Docker and Kubernetes CRI, just to name the most popular ones. It is available as a daemon for Linux and Windows, which can manage the complete container life cycle of its host system, including container image management, container execution, low-level storage, and network attachments.

Moby
> Moby is a set of open source tools created by Docker to enable and accelerate software containerization. The toolkit includes container build tools, a container registry, orchestration tools, a runtime, and more, and you can use these as building blocks in conjunction with other tools and projects. Moby is using containerd as the default container runtime.

Serverless Computing

Serverless computing means that scale and the underlying infrastructure is managed by the cloud provider; that is, your application automatically drives the allocation and deallocation of resources, and you do not need to worry about managing the underlying infrastructure at all. All management and operations are abstracted away from the user and managed by cloud providers such as Microsoft Azure, Amazon Web Services (AWS), and Google Cloud Platform (GCP). From a developer perspective, serverless often adds an event-driven programming model, and from an economic perspective, you pay only per execution (CPU time consumed).

Many people think Function as a Service (FaaS) is serverless. This is technically true, but FaaS is only one variation of serverless computing. Microsoft Azure's Container Instances (ACI) and Azure SF Mesh, as well as AWS Fargate and GCP's Serverless Containers on Cloud Functions, are good examples. ACI and AWS Fargate are serverless container offerings also known as Container as a Service (CaaS), which allow you to deploy containerized applications without needing to know about the underlying infrastructure. Other examples of serverless offerings are API management and machine learning services—basically, any service that lets you consume functionality without managing the underlying infrastructure and a pay-only-for-what-you-use model qualifies as serverless offering.

Functions

When talking about functions, people typically talk about FaaS offerings such as AWS Lambda, Azure Functions, and Google Cloud Functions, which are implemented on serverless infrastructure. The advantages of serverless computing—fast startup and execution time, plus the simplification of their applications—makes FaaS offerings very compelling to developers because it allows them to focus solely on writing code.

From a development perspective, a function is the unit of work, which means that your code has a start and a finish. Functions are usually triggered by events that are emitted by either other functions or platform services. For example, a function can be triggered by adding an entry to a database service or eventing service. There are quite a few things to consider when you want to build a large, complex application just with functions. You will need to manage more independent code, you will need to ensure state is being taken care of, and you will need to implement patterns if functions must depend on one another, just to name a few. Containerized microservices share a lot of the same patterns, so there have been quite a few discussions around when to use FaaS or a container. Table 2-1 provides some high-level guidance between FaaS and containers, and Chapter 3 covers the trade-offs in more detail.

Table 2-1. Comparison of FaaS and containerized services

FaaS	Containerized service
Does one thing	Does more than one thing
Can't deploy dependencies	Can deploy dependencies
Must respond to one kind of event	Can respond to more than one kind of event

There are two scenarios in which using FaaS offerings might not be ideal, although it offers the best economics. First, you want to avoid vendor lock-in. Because you need to develop your function specific to the FaaS offering and consume higher-level cloud services from a provider, your entire application becomes less portable. Second, you want to run functions on-premises or your own clusters. There are a bunch of FaaS runtimes that are available as open source runtimes and that you can run on any Kubernetes cluster. Kubeless, OpenFaaS, Serverless, and Apache OpenWhisk are among the most popular installable FaaS platforms, with Azure Functions gaining more popularity since it has been open sourced. Installable FaaS platforms are typically deployed through containers and allow the developer to simply deploy small bits of code (functions) without needing to worry about the underlying infrastructure. Many installable FaaS frameworks use Kubernetes resources for routing, autoscaling, and monitoring.

A critical aspect of any FaaS implementation, no matter whether it runs on a cloud provider's serverless infrastructure or is installed on your own clusters, is the startup time. In general, you expect functions to execute very quickly after they have been triggered, which implies that their underlying technology needs to provide very fast boot-up times. As previously discussed, containers provide good startup times, but do not necessarily offer the best isolation.

From VMs to Cloud Native

To understand how we ended up with the next generation of cloud native applications, it is worth looking at how applications evolve from running on VMs to functions. Describing the journey should give you a good idea of how the IT industry is changing to put developer productivity into focus and how you can take advantage of all the new technologies. There are really two different paths to the cloud native world. The first one is mainly used for *brownfield scenarios*, which means that you have an existing application, and typically follows a lift-and-shift, application modernization, and eventually an application optimization process. The second one is a *greenfield scenario* in which you start your application from scratch.

Lift-and-Shift

Installing software directly on machines in the cloud is still the very first step for many customers to move to the cloud. The benefits are mainly in the capital and operational expense areas given that customers do not need to operate their own datacenters or can at least reduce operations and, therefore, the costs. From a technical perspective, lift-and-shift into Infrastructure as a Service (IaaS) gives you the most control over the entire stack. With control comes responsibility, and installing software directly on machines often resulted in errors caused by missing dependencies, runtime versioning conflicts, resource contention, and isolation. The next logical step is to move applications into a Platform as a Service (PaaS) environment. PaaS existed long before containers became popular; for example, Azure Cloud Services dates back to 2010. In most past PaaS environments, access to the underlying VMs is restricted or in some cases prohibited so that moving to the cloud requires some rewriting of the applications. The benefit for developers is not to worry about the underlying infrastructure anymore. Operational tasks such as patching the OS were handled by the cloud providers, but some of the problems, like missing dependencies, remained. Because many PaaS services were based on VMs, scaling in burst scenarios was still a challenge due to the downsides of VMs, which we discussed previously, and for economic reasons.

Application Modernization

Besides offering super-fast startup times, containers drastically removed the issues of missing dependencies, because everything an application needed is packaged inside a container. It didn't take long for developers to begin to love the concept of containers as a packaging format, and now pretty much every new application is using containers, and more and more monolithic legacy applications are being containerized. Many customers see the containerization of an existing application as an opportunity to also move to a more suitable architecture for cloud native environments. Microservices is the obvious choice, but as you will see later in the chapter, moving to such an architecture comes with some disadvantages. There are a few very obvious reasons, though, why you want to break up your monolith:

- Time to deployment is faster.
- Certain components need to update more frequently than others.
- Certain components need different scale requirements.
- Certain components should be developed in a different technology.
- The codebase has gotten too big and complex.

Although the methodology to break up a monolith goes beyond the scope of this book, it is worth mentioning the two major patterns to move from a monolithic application to microservices.

Strangler pattern
   With the Strangler pattern, you strangle the monolithic application. New services or existing components are implemented as microservices. A facade or gateway routes user requests to the correct application. Over time, more and more features are moved to the new architecture until the monolithic application has been entirely transformed into a microservices application.

Anticorruption Layer pattern

> This is similar to the Strangler pattern but is used when new services need to access the legacy application. The layer then translates the concepts from existing app to new, and vice versa.

We describe both patterns in more detail in Chapter 6.

With applications being packaged in container images, orchestrators began to play a more important role. Even though there were several choices in the beginning, Kubernetes has become the most popular choice today; in fact, it is considered the new cloud OS. Orchestrators, however, added another variable to the equation insomuch as development and operations teams needed to understand them. The management part of the environment has become better, as pretty much every cloud vendor now offers "orchestrators" as a service. As with any cloud provider, "managed" Kubernetes means that the setup and runtime part of the Kubernetes service is managed. From an economical point of view, users are typically being charged for compute hours, which means that you pay as long as the nodes of the cluster are up and running even though the application might be sitting idle or utilizing low resources.

From a developer perspective, you still need to understand how Kubernetes works if you want to build microservices applications on top of it given that Kubernetes does not offer any PaaS or CaaS features out of the box.

For example, a Kubernetes service does not really represent the service code within a container, it just provides an endpoint to it, so that the code within the container can always be accessed through the same endpoint. In addition to needing to understand Kubernetes, developers are also being introduced to distributed systems patterns to handle resiliency, diagnostics, and routing, just to name a few.

Service meshes such as Istio or Linkerd are gaining popularity because they are moving some of the distributed systems complexity into the platform layer. Chapter 3 covers service meshes in great detail, but for now you can think of a service mesh as being a dedicated networking infrastructure layer that handles the service-to-service communication. Among other things, service meshes enable resiliency features such as retries and circuit breakers, distributed tracing, and routing.

The next step of application evolution is to use serverless infrastructure for containerized workloads, aka CaaS offerings such as Azure Container Instances or AWS Fargate. Microsoft Azure has done a great job to meld the world of its managed Kubernetes Service (AKS) with its CaaS offering, ACI, by using *virtual nodes*. Virtual nodes is based on Microsoft's open source project called Virtual Kubelet, which allows any compute resource to act as a Kubernetes node and use the Kubernetes control plane. In the case of AKS virtual nodes, you are able to schedule your application on AKS and burst into ACI without needing to set up additional nodes in case your cluster cannot offer any more resources in a scale-out scenario. Figure 2-6 shows how an existing monolithic application (Legacy App) is broken down into smaller microservices (Feature 3). The legacy application and the new microservice (Feature 3) are on a service mesh on Kubernetes. In this case Feature 3 has independent scale needs and can be scaled out into a CaaS offering using Virtual Kubelet.

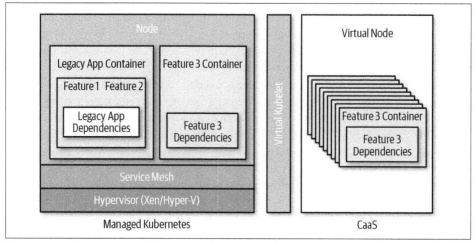

Figure 2-6. Modernized application with Feature 3 being scaled out into CaaS using Virtual Kubelet

Application Optimization

The next step is to improve the application in terms not only of further cost optimization, but also of code optimization. Functions really excel in short-lived compute scenarios, such as updating records, sending emails, transforming messages, and so on. To take advantage of functions, you can identify short-lived compute functionality in your service codebase and implement it using functions. A good example is an order service in which the containerized microservice does all the Create, Read, Update, and Delete (CRUD) operations, and a function sends the notification of a successfully placed order. To trigger the function, eventing or messaging systems are being used. Eventually, you could decide to build the entire order service using functions, with each function executing one of the CRUD operations.

Microservices

Microservices is a term commonly used to refer to a microservices architecture style, or the individual services in a microservices architecture. A microservices architecture is a service-oriented architecture in which applications are decomposed into small, loosely coupled services by area of functionality. It's important that services remain relatively small, are loosely coupled, and are decomposed around business capability.

Microservices architectures are often compared and contrasted with monolithic architectures. Instead of managing a single codebase, a shared datastore, and data structure, as in a monolith, in a microservices architecture an application is composed of smaller codebases, created and managed by independent teams. Each service is owned and operated by a small team, with all elements of the service contributing to a single well-defined task. Services run in separate processes and communicate through APIs that are either synchronous or asynchronous message based.

Each service can be viewed as its very own application with an independent team, tests, builds, data, and deployments. Figure 2-7 shows the concept of a microservices architecture, using the Inventory service as an example.

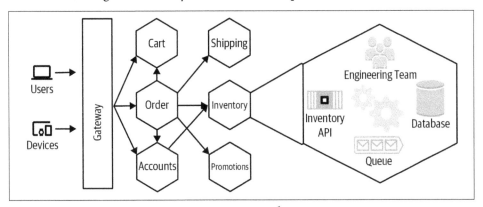

Figure 2-7. Inventory service in a microservices architecture

Benefits of a Microservices Architecture

A properly implemented microservices architecture will increase the release velocity of large applications, enabling businesses to deliver value to customers faster and more reliably.

Agility

Fast, reliable deployments can be challenging with large, monolithic applications. A deployment of a small change to a module in one feature area can be held up by a change to another feature. As an application grows, testing of the application will increase and it can take a considerable amount of time to deliver new value to stakeholders. A change to one feature will require the entire application to be redeployed and rolled forward or back if there is an issue with that change. By decomposing an application into smaller services, the time needed to verify and release changes can be reduced and deployed more reliably.

Continuous innovation

Companies need to move increasingly faster in order to remain relevant today. This requires organizations to be agile and capable of quickly adapting to fast-changing market conditions. Companies can no longer wait years or months to deliver new value to customers: they must often deliver new value daily. A microservices architecture can make it easier to deliver value to stakeholders in a reliable way. Small independent teams are able to release features and perform A/B testing to improve conversions or user experience during even the busiest times.

Evolutionary design

With a large monolithic application, it can be very difficult to adopt new technologies or techniques because this will often require that the entire application be rewritten or care needs to be taken to ensure that some new dependency can run side-by-side with a previous one. Loose coupling and high functional cohesion is important to a system design that is able to evolve through changing technologies. By decomposing an application by features into small, loosely coupled services, it can be much easier to change individual services without affecting the entire application. Different languages, frameworks, and libraries can be used across the different services if needed to support the business.

Small, focused teams

Structuring engineering teams at scale and keeping them focused and productive can be challenging. Making people responsible for designing, running, and operating what they build can also be challenging if what you are building is heavily intertwined with what everyone else is building. It can sometimes take new team members days, weeks, or even months to get up to speed and begin contributing because they are burdened with understanding aspects of a system that are unrelated to their area of focus. By decomposing an application into smaller services, small agile teams are able to focus on a smaller concern and move quickly. It can be much easier for a new member joining because they need to be concerned with only a smaller service. Team members can more easily operate and take accountability for the services they build.

Fault isolation

In a monolithic application, a single library or module can cause problems for the entire application. A memory leak in one module not only can affect the stability and performance of the entire application, but can often be difficult to isolate and identify. By decomposing features of the application into independent services, teams can isolate a defect in one service to that service.

Improved scale and resource usage

Applications are generally scaled up or out. They are scaled up by increasing the size or type of machine, and scaled out by increasing the number of instances deployed and routing users across these instances. Different features of an application will sometimes have different resource requirements; for example, memory, CPU, disk, and so on. Application features will often have different scale requirements. Some features might easily scale out with very few resources required for each instance, whereas other features might require large amounts of memory with limited ability to scale out. By decoupling these features into independent services, teams can configure the services to run in environments that best meet the services, individual resource and scale requirements.

Improved observability

In a monolithic application it can be difficult to measure and observe the individual components of an application without careful and detailed instrumentation throughout the application. By decomposing features of an application into separate services, teams can use tools to gain deeper insights into the behavior of the individual features and interactions with other features. System metrics such as process utilization and memory usage can now easily be tied back to the feature team because it's running in a separate process or container.

Challenges with a Microservices Architecture

Despite all the benefits of a microservices architecture, there are trade-offs, and a microservices architecture does have its own set of challenges. Tooling and technologies have begun to address some of these challenges, but many of them still remain. A microservices architecture might not be the best choice for all applications today, but we can still apply many of the concepts and practices to other architectures. The best approach often lies somewhere in between.

Complexity

Distributed systems are inherently complex. As we decompose the application into individual services, network calls are necessary for the individual services to communicate. Networks calls add latency and experience transient failures, and the operations can run on different machines with a different clock, each having a slightly different sense of the current time. We cannot assume that the network is reliable, latency is zero, bandwidth is infinite, the network is secure, the topology will not change, there is one administrator, transport costs are zero, and that the network is homogenous. Many developers are not familiar with distributed systems and often make false assumptions when entering that world. The *Fallacies of Distributed Computing*, as discussed in Chapter 1, is a set of assertions describing those false assumptions commonly made by developers. They were first documented by L. Peter

Deutsch and other Sun Microsystems engineers and are covered in numerous blog articles. Chapter 6 provides more information about best practices, tools, and techniques for dealing with the complexities of distributed systems.

Data integrity and consistency

Decentralized data means that data will often exist in multiple places with relationships spanning different systems. Performing transactions across these systems can be difficult, and we need to employ a different approach to data management. One service might have a relationship to data in another service; for example, an order service might have a reference to a customer in an account service. Data might have been copied from the account service in order to satisfy some performance requirements. If the customer is removed or disabled, it can be important that the order service is updated to indicate this status. Dealing with data will require a different approach. Chapter 4 covers patterns for dealing with this.

Performance

Networking requests and data serialization add overhead. In a microservices-based architecture the number of network requests will increase. Remember, components are libraries that are no longer making direct calls; this is happening over a network. A call to one service can result in a call to another dependent service. It might take a number of requests to multiple services in order to satisfy the original request. We can implement some patterns and best practices to mitigate potential performance overhead in a microservices architecture, which we look at in Chapter 6.

Development and testing

Development can be a bit more challenging because the tools and practices used today don't work with a microservices architecture. Given the velocity of change and the fact that there are many more external dependencies, it can be challenging to run a complete test suite on versions of the dependent services that will be running in production. We can implement a different approach to testing to address these challenges, and a proper Continuous Integration/Continuous Deployment (CI/CD) pipeline will be necessary. Development tooling and test strategies have evolved over the years to better accommodate a microservices architecture. Chapter 5 covers many of the tools, techniques, and best practices.

Versioning and integration

Changing an interface in a monolithic application can require some refactoring, but the changes are often built, tested, and deployed as a single cohesive unit. In a microservices architecture service, dependencies are changing and evolving independently of the consumers. Careful attention to forward and backward compatibility is necessary when dealing with service versioning. In addition to maintaining forward and backward compatibility with service changes, it might be possible to deploy an entirely new version of the service, running it side-by-side with the previous version for some period of time. Chapter 5 explores service versioning and integration strategies.

Monitoring and logging

Many organizations struggle with monitoring and logging of monolithic applications, even when they are using a common shared logging library. Inconsistencies in naming, data types, and values make it difficult to correlate relevant log events. In a microservices architecture, when relevant events span multiple services—all potentially using different logging implementations—correlating these events can be even more challenging. Planning and early attention to the importance of logging and monitoring can help address much of this, which we examine in Chapter 5.

Service dependency management

With a monolithic application, dependencies on libraries are generally compiled into a single package and tested. In a microservices architecture, service dependencies are managed differently, requiring environment-specific routing and discovery. Service discovery and routing tools and technologies have come a long way in addressing these challenges. Chapter 3 looks at these in depth.

Availability

Although a microservices architecture can help isolate faults to individual services, if other services or the application as a whole is unable to function without that service, the application will be unavailable. As the number of services increases, the chance that one of those services experiences a failure also increases. Services will need to implement resilient design patterns, or some functionality downgraded in the event of a service outage. Chapter 6 covers patterns and best practices for building highly available applications and provides more detail on the specific challenges.

Summary

Every application, whether cloud native or traditional, needs infrastructure on which to be hosted, technology that addresses pain points with development and deployment, and an architectural style that helps with achieving the business objectives, such as time to market. The goal of this chapter was to provide the basic knowledge for cloud native applications. By now you should understand that there are various container technologies with different isolation levels, how functions relate to containers, and that serverless infrastructure does not always need to be FaaS. Further, you should have a basic understanding of microservices architectures and of how you can migrate and modernize an existing application to be a cloud native application.

The upcoming chapters build on this knowledge and go deep into how to design, develop, and operate cloud native applications.

CHAPTER 3

Designing Cloud Native Applications

Application architectures are a result of unique business requirements, which makes it difficult to come up with an architectural blueprint that is generally applicable. Cloud native applications are no exception to that. A good way to approach designing cloud native applications is to consider five key areas when starting with the initial design: operational excellence, security, reliability, scalability, and cost. From an actual implementation perspective there are certain building blocks, patterns, and technologies that are proven to be very useful in solving specific problems. Besides discussing these five key areas, this chapter also covers the most common architectural building blocks.

The goal of this chapter is to equip you with the knowledge necessary to design and build cloud native architectures effectively.

Fundamentals of Cloud Native Applications

All the major cloud providers offer guidance on how to build applications targeting their respective cloud environments. Microsoft Azure has its cloud application architecture and cloud patterns guide, Amazon Web Services (AWS) has its well-architected framework, and Google offers various guides on how to build cloud native applications. Although those guides are more specific to their services offered in each environment, you can identify five generally applicable pillars that you should keep in mind regardless of the cloud provider you are choosing.

Operational Excellence

Operational excellence means that you need to factor in how to run your application, monitor it, and improve it over time when you are starting to design. *Build, measure,* and *learn* are verbs often used to describe the process, and DevOps is the way to implement it. Chapter 5 covers many of the operational excellence principles in detail, but it is still worthwhile to provide a high-level overview of the pillars as part of this chapter because they play a fundamental role in designing a cloud native application:

Automate everything

Cloud automation goes hand in hand with Infrastructure as Code (IaC). This enables you to minimize errors during environment provisioning and application deployment because the entire environment management is being defined using code artifacts. Azure Resource Manager and AWS CloudFormation are good examples. Chapter 7 also briefly discusses HashiCorp's Terraform, which enables you to use the same IaC approach across multiple cloud vendors. Besides minimizing errors, automation also enables you to track changes to your environment through source code control systems as well as quickly spinning up new environments in a consistent way. Besides automating how to provision the environments, you also need to automate the entire deployment process of your application.

Monitor everything

Monitoring allows you to learn not only about your application and environment behavior, but also how your application is being used. Based on the monitoring data you can take action to improve operational costs, performance, and the functionality of an application. From an architectural point of view you need to ensure that you have consistent monitoring across the entire stack, starting from the infrastructure hosting the services you use all the way to the features and functionality of your application. As mentioned previously, Chapter 5 provides details on how to accomplish consistent monitoring for the entire stack, including the application.

Document everything

It is very common that cloud native applications are being built by many teams. As you have seen in previous chapters, microservices architectures are promoting the idea of small independent teams building individual services. Although documentation is important in any software development project, it is crucial in cloud native applications. Every team member needs to be able to understand how they can consume services built by other teams, or everyone should be able to understand how the environment is defined and provisioned. Documentation should be done automatically and not manually. A good example is using an OpenAPI specification for your service APIs. This allows you to automatically generate documentation for your service API through check-ins given that you can use the Swagger tools as part of a Continuous Integration (CI) step.

Make incremental changes

When making changes to both the environment as well as the application, you need to ensure that those changes are incremental and reversible. This leads back to one of the advantages of using IaC. Because your environment description and definition should reside in a source control repository, you can easily reverse any change.

Design for failure

Failures in the cloud will happen—period. You need to think not only about how to design your application to survive failures, but also about about the processes that need to kick in when something goes wrong. There are many testing frameworks available that help you to simulate failures, helping you to learn what the impact is and to plan to mitigate those failures.

Security

All the major cloud providers employ an army of security experts who ensure that their environments are super secure. By now it has become an accepted fact that cloud environments are safer than most on-premises environments. Just because the cloud environments are relatively safe does not mean that you can and should ignore the security of your applications. Because cloud native architectures typically consist of many components, the *defense-in-depth* concept has been proven to be best suited for securing your applications. Defense-in-depth means that security controls are implemented throughout your architecture. Although security for cloud native applications is beyond the scope of this book, it's important to take a brief moment to understand what defense-in-depth means for your cloud native application. Let's begin by looking at a simple cloud native application, as shown in Figure 3-1.

The functionality of this application is explained later in this chapter. For the defense-in-depth discussions, it is enough to understand that the voting application uses containerized services running on an orchestrator, an eventing system, Function as a Service (FaaS), and a Datastore as a Service (DaaS).

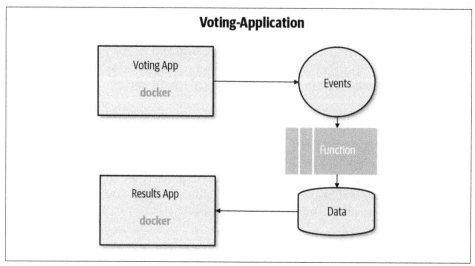

Figure 3-1. A simple application

The following is a defense-in-depth list of containerized services, assuming you are using Kubernetes as the orchestrator:

Source code
Ensure that you are using a secure code repository and that you track and audit access to it. As part of your CI step, you can check your code for vulnerabilities, especially kernel exploits if you use Linux containers.

Container image
Ensure that you always add only what is necessary to the base image and that you expose only the ports that are absolutely needed.

Container registry
You should use a private registry with which you can track and audit who has access to the registry using Role-Based Access Control (RBAC) polices. You should also scan your images for vulnerabilities using tools like Twistlock.

Pod
Ensure that container images can be pulled only from approved registries. In Kubernetes, you can use policy controllers to implement such policies. Make sure your pod has an identity so that the code within it can access other services in a secure manner. You should also think about whether you need to secure the service-to-service communication within your cluster. As you will see later, service meshes are great solutions for that.

Cluster and orchestrator
> You need to determine whether your cluster that is hosting the orchestrator needs to be accessed over the internet or whether a VPN is sufficient. You also need to secure access to the control plane of the orchestrator and enable audit logs. You can use network policies to secure the communication paths between nodes and namespaces. Finally, make sure Kubernetes has RBAC enabled.

For the service-to-service communication within the application—for example, the voting service accessing the messaging service—you need to ensure that the data in transit is protected and that only authenticated services are granted access. In the example of the voting service, only the voting app pod's identity should be allowed to access the messaging service. The same principles—protect the data and secure the communication between services—apply to the other services in the voting application.

This is by no means a complete list, but it should give you a sense of how to think about a defense-in-depth approach.

Reliability and Availability

Reliability and availability are discussed throughout this book, but it might still be useful to understand how they relate to each other.

Reliability means that the application will still work in an acceptable way even in the presence of failure, whereas *availability* means that your application is available for a certain amount of time.

From a reliability perspective, you need to ensure that your application is designed in a way that it can recover from failure. As you have seen, microservices architectures help in a way that each service is independent and does not take down the entire application in case of a failure. For the service itself, you should think about scaling horizontally to increase the aggregated system availability. For example, if you run two instances of any service, you improve its reliability in case one instance fails for any reason. We have already touched on the fact that the network is not reliable, so you should also consider retries and circuit breakers as part of your design. Both are discussed in detail as part of "Service Mesh" on page 59.

In summary, to design for reliability and availability you should have testing in place that informs you of how your system is behaving and how your recovery mechanisms work. And, of course, the application needs to recover automatically by taking advantage of the scaling capabilities.

Scalability and Cost

Scalability and cost go hand in hand. When designing a cloud native application, you need to think about not only how to scale the application, but also how to do it in a very cost-efficient way. Let's think about the voting application again. One way to implement it is to deploy the voting app and the result app to a managed Kubernetes cluster. Pretty much all managed Kubernetes services require you to define the number of nodes you need at the outset, so you need to determine what your maximal load will be and how many nodes you need to handle the maximal anticipated traffic. This decision has a direct impact on your cost given that you need to size your cluster in a way that it can host all of the instances of the voting and results application under load. This is not very cost effective, because most of the time the application might not utilize all of the nodes.

One solution could be to go with fewer nodes and rely on horizontal node autoscalers if the existing number of nodes cannot provide sufficient resources for all instances anymore. The problem with that design is that spinning up new nodes usually takes longer than just spinning up new containers, so it is not super useful in unpredictable burst scenarios. There are a couple of options for how to implement the solution; for example, burst into Container as a Service (CaaS) offerings such as Azure Kubernetes Service virtual node or AWS Fargate. A good way to design your solution in a scalable and cost-efficient way is to experiment during development and even in production. Chapter 5 provides a detailed overview of testing cloud native applications.

Cloud Native versus Traditional Architectures

Chapter 2 examined cloud native and microservices architectures and their pros and cons, but it is also useful to point out some differences from traditional architectures.

One of the fundamental differences between cloud native applications and traditional *monolithic* applications is how state—that is, session state, application and configuration data, and so on—is handled. *Traditional applications* are often stateful in nature, which means that the application state was commonly stored with the compute instance. For that very reason, load balancers were using sticky sessions to make sure that a user request always ended up on the same server instance. A good example for statefulness is session state. With traditional applications, it was quite common to retrieve user-specific data, such as user profile information, from an external data-store and store it in session variables. The load balancer ensured that all of the traffic from the user ended up on the same instance. Figure 3-2 shows a request (1) coming from a client to the load balancer. The load balancer establishes a session with the first virtual machine (VM). Application Instance 0 now loads the state and serves the request.

In case of a failure, such as VM reboot, network connection loss, or application instance crash, the load balancer detects that the first VM is no longer reachable and establishes a new session on the second VM for the user (2). Application Instance 1 has no state information because the state was stored on the first VM. This can lead not only to user dissatisfaction, but also to inconsistencies in state.

Cloud native applications, on the other hand, are stateless by nature. Stateless does not mean that they do not deal with data, but it means that they need to be designed in a way that the number of compute instances is highly dynamic without affecting user experiences that rely on data. In cloud native architectures, state is usually externalized, meaning that the data is stored in state stores such as storage services. Chapter 4 provides a deep dive into working with data.

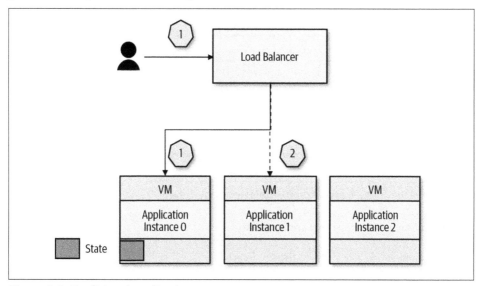

Figure 3-2. Traditional application

Figure 3-3 shows a request to an application with externalized state.

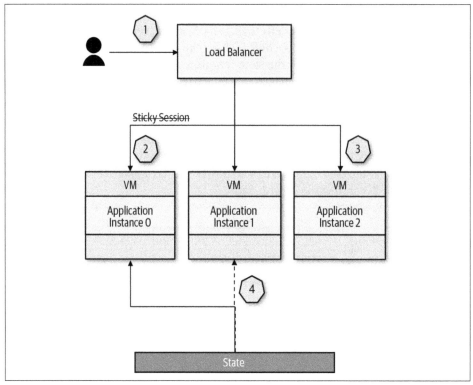

Figure 3-3. Cloud native application with externalized state

Here's what's happening in this application:

1. The client sends a request to the application.
2. The load balancer randomly routes the request to Application Instance 0, which reads and writes the state to an external state store.
3. In case of a failure of Application Instance 0, the load balancer sends the requests from the client to Application Instance 2.
4. Application Instance 2 reads the state for the initial request from the external state store and the client is not affected by the failure at all.

You also can see how keeping your services stateless helps with dynamic scaling in and out. The system can just add and remove instances, scaling out and in, without affecting the user experience (UX).

One word of caution for scaling-in scenarios: most of the time you are responsible for ensuring that all connections are drained of the instance before scaling in.

In addition, monolithic applications often use *service orchestration* as the most common integration technique between different components. Service orchestration, not to be confused with *container orchestration* on Kubernetes, is a technique whereby multiple components or services are orchestrated to work as one. The services typically use synchronous communication. (Synchronous communication and request/response patterns are explained later in this chapter.) Figure 3-4 shows an application using service orchestration.

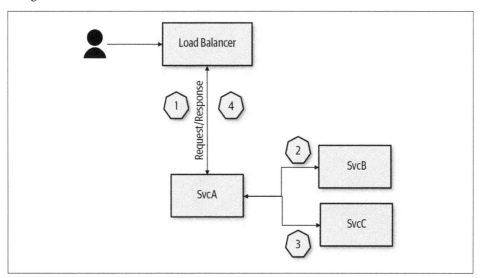

Figure 3-4. Service orchestration

Let's take a closer look at this application:

1. The client sends a request to the application. The request is routed through the load balancer to Service A (SvcA).

2. SvcA sends a request to both Service B (SvcB) and Service C (SvcC) and waits for their response.

3. After SvcB and SvcC send their responses back, Svc A will respond to the client.

Cloud native applications often use event-driven patterns for communication. Organizing requests across loosely coupled services is called *service choreography*. With service choreography, each service is isolated, autonomous, and responsible for managing its own state, which are some of the characteristics of microservices-based applications. Figure 3-5 demonstrates service choreography.

Again, let's see how this application works:

1. The client sends a request to the application. The request is routed through the load balancer to SvcA, and SvcA requests data for the user request from the messaging system.

2. SvcB acts independently and sends its data to an eventing system.

3. SvcC acts independently and sends its data to an eventing system.

4. SvcA picks up the data from the eventing system and sends it back to the client.

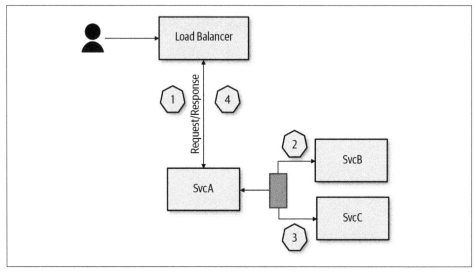

Figure 3-5. Service choreography

The communication for service orchestration and service choreography are described in more detail in the sections "Request/Response" on page 49 and "Publisher/Subscriber" on page 51.

Finally, there is a big difference in how cloud native architectures deal with failures as opposed to how traditional applications cope with them. As mentioned earlier, cloud native architectures expect failures and implement mechanisms to deal with them, whereas traditional architectures try to minimize failures; for example, through database clustering and so on.

Functions versus Services

One of the very first decisions that you must make when building a new application, or even when moving an existing application to a cloud native application, is whether you should use a containerized service (for the remainder of the chapter, we refer to it simply as a *service*) or move straight to FaaS. Chapter 2 provided some high-level guidance on when to use functions versus services. In a nutshell, you should consider using FaaS for simple, short-lived, and independent tasks, but many FaaS offerings have matured in a way that you can implement entire applications using FaaS. One limiting factor is that most FaaS offerings still impose a timeout on the execution time of a function.

Function Scenarios

The following is a list of scenarios for which functions are a good fit:

- Simple parallel execution scenarios in which functions do not need to communicate with one another. Sample scenarios include generation of artifacts, updating records, map-reduce functions, and batch processing.

- Many Internet of Things (IoT) scenarios use functions for orchestration tasks. For example, messages are sent to an IoT hub, which triggers functions to perform some computing and routing tasks on a message.

- Some applications are entirely built using FaaS offerings, meaning that the complete application is built using functions. Azure Durable Functions or AWS Step Functions are function types that enable you to build an entire application using function primitives. Those function types also help with orchestrating longer-running tasks in an application.

Considerations for Using Functions

There are several considerations that you need to keep in mind when building an entire application using functions:

Challenges when moving from a monolith to microservices
Because functions are typically broken down into even smaller "services," you generally need to deal with a multiplier of those challenges, such as network communication complexity.

Limited lifetime of a function
As mentioned previously, most FaaS offerings limit the execution time of a function, which means that they are not suited for long-running tasks.

No usage of specialized hardware

As of this writing, there is no cloud offering for a function to take advantage of specialized hardware such as graphics processing units (GPUs), which are superior to standard CPUs for training models for machine learning applications.

Functions are stateless and not directly network addressable

For that reason, FaaS encourages an event-driven distributed programming model or the use of API management solutions to front functions. Typically, functions work together by passing data through eventing or messaging systems. The state is stored in cloud services, which means event handling requires moving pieces of the state from storage into and out of stateless functions. This incurs networking latency with every hop. Overall, you can see how a large application built solely by functions can suffer a performance loss as a result of all of the communication and data being processed over the network.

Local development and debugging

Local development and debugging is not available for all the FaaS offerings, because some of the FaaS runtimes are not portable.

Economics

Although you save on compute costs, FaaS offerings typically charge for execution time; thus, you need to factor in increased costs for networking and other cloud services such as storage and eventing. There are scenarios for which applications implemented entirely on FaaS are more expensive; unfortunately, planning and predicting the costs of FaaS remain very challenging.

Composite of Functions and Services

Services packaged in containers, on the other hand, do not have a limit on the execution time. Besides, you can use specialized hardware; for instance, many managed Kubernetes services allow you to build clusters with specialized hardware such as GPUs. You can also create services using local persistent storage, which limits the network hops your application needs to make.

Most of the time a combination of functions and services is a great solution allowing you to take advantage of the simplicity of FaaS while benefitting from the flexibility of containerized services. Figure 3-6 shows the previously introduced voting application using this hybrid approach.

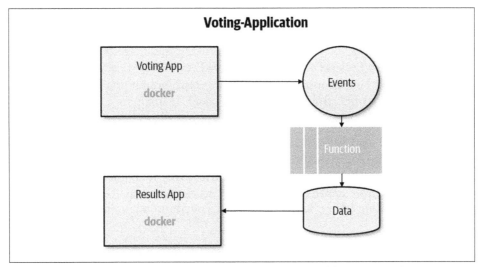

Figure 3-6. Simple voting application using a combination of functions and services

The voting app is a containerized service that allows users to submit votes. After a vote is submitted, the message is placed into an eventing system. The eventing system triggers functions that add the data to a datastore based on some header information, such as device type. The results application reads the data from the datastore and displays the voting results. The pattern implemented here is also known as an *Event Sourcing* pattern.

Implementing the logic to add data to the datastore as a function allows the application to easily scale when needed and also to run in the most economical way.

Serverless cloud native applications are very dynamic, meaning new pods or functions can spin up and down based on demand or failures. The scale out and scale in, meaning adding more service instances (pods) or functions or decreasing the number, is usually provided by the cloud provider. Your responsibility is to design your application in a way that it can handle those scenarios. For instance, if your application stores its state locally, it will lose the state when the pod is moved or new functions are spun up due to the statefulness nature, as mentioned at the beginning of this chapter.

The recommended best practice for this case is to push that data into highly available managed services, such as a Relational Database Management System (RDBMS) or caching services. You also can deploy stateful applications on Kubernetes by using Stateful Sets, which use persistent volumes. (Chapter 4 covers Kubernetes Stateful Sets in more detail.)

You also need to understand how your application scales. Cloud providers make it very easy to scale your cloud native applications, but you are still responsible for thinking about what happens when the application scales. For example, if you use large container images and you expect your application to quickly scale in burst scenarios, you are setting yourself up for failure. Pulling the image onto another node can take some time because a large package needs to be downloaded over the wire. The download can take a considerable amount of time, even if this happens within a cloud provider network from a private container registry to a cluster or CaaS offering.

Even though cold-start behavior, which is the time it takes to launch a function or a container, is usually not so much a problem for FaaS offerings, you might still need to understand the scale behavior. In a burst scenario, many functions will run concurrently, and if you have dependencies on other services such as RDBMS, you might max out your connections, which will ultimately result in a slowdown of your application.

The bottom line is that even with the cloud provider's autoscaling capabilities, you are not off the hook, and you still need to understand how your application scales.

API Design and Versioning

Because the API is the interface other services use to communicate with your service, it is important to properly document and version your APIs. The reality is that API versioning is difficult, especially given that there are different approaches that you can take. Based on the research done by Jean-Jacques Dubray, the cost of developing your API depends on the strategy you take. He classified three different strategies:

The knot
Consumers of your API are tied to a single version of the API. When the API changes, all consumers need to change as well. This is the most expensive approach for the consumers because they are forced to upgrade each time a new API version is released.

Point-to-point
All API versions are kept running and each consumer uses the version they need to. Consumers can migrate to the new versions when they decide to. Compared to the knot, this is a bit better strategy for the consumers, but it is costly for the API developer to maintain older API versions.

Compatible versioning
All consumers talk to the same API version. Old versions are deprecated and no longer exist because the latest version is backward compatible.

The results from the research have shown that the *compatible versioning* strategy offers the best efficiency. It does introduce more work for the API developer in order to maintain backward compatibility.

REST doesn't provide any specific versioning, but there are three approaches that deal with versioning: *global versioning, resource versioning,* and *mime-based approach.* Each one of these approaches has its pros and cons, and there is no clear and best approach here.

With global versioning, you version the entire API and the version is part of the path (e.g., */api/v1/users*) or a subdomain (e.g., *api-v1.example.com/users*). If the representation of the user changes, you create a new version of the full API, even though other resources might not have changed at all. Creating a new version of the API with every breaking change gives you, the developer, a clearer and easier way to get rid of the old API versions. However, there are downsides to this approach. The API consumers are constantly pushed to move to the newer versions as they are released, and there's a significant cost in testing and maintaining multiple versions, and this takes a lot of time.

An approach that gives you a more granular versioning story is to use resource versioning. Very similar to the global version, but in this case, you are versioning specific resources. That way, if the user's resource changes, you can create a new version of that specific resource (e.g., */api/v2/users*); however, the other resources would remain unchanged (e.g., */api/v1/tasks*).

Both of these approaches have the API versions either in the URL path or the domain. With the mime-based approach, you are still versioning on the resource level; however, you are not including the version number in the URL but in the headers instead. For example, you use the Accept and Content-Type headers to describe the resource version and its type (e.g., Accept: *application/vnd.example.users.v2+json*), whereas the URL stays versionless (e.g., */api/users*). This means that your API endpoints stay clean, but it could make using the API more complicated.

Regardless of the aforementioned REST versioning approaches, a bigger challenge to the API versioning is the way you are managing your code that can support different multiple resource versions. You don't want your versioning to be so strict that it prevents you from making changes to the API. On the other hand, you also need to maintain the stable contract. As a part of your strategy, you should understand how to manage changes to the API while still providing a stable contract to the clients.

Using the compatible versioning strategy, your APIs are backward compatible and different clients can all talk to one version of the API. Because different clients can talk to the same API version, there's no need to maintain a separate API version for each client.

In addition to the client and the server (the API implementation) version, you also need to version the message formats as well as the API documentation. Note that you don't version the resources, relations between the resources, or the API itself.

When introducing changes to the API you need to consider the backward and potentially forward compatibility of the API. For example, if you are changing the URI (e.g., query parameters) or modifying the headers or body of the message and these changes violate or break the backward compatibility, you need to either create a new resource or use content negotiation if the message format changed.

Regardless of the approach you take, it is important that you are able to monitor the API and versions of the API used by the consumers. Having good monitoring in place helps you decide how and when to deprecate the APIs.

API Backward and Forward Compatibility

Before going into the service communication options, let's go over a quick refresher on API compatibility. Because you will be deploying services autonomously and independently from one another, you need to ensure that updates to your service don't break existing services with which you are communicating. If you are applying the compatible versioning strategy explained earlier, your services need to be backward and forward compatible. Figure 3-7 shows Service A v1.0 working together with Service B v1.0.

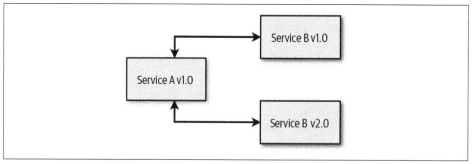

Figure 3-7. Backward compatibility

Now you deploy Service B v2.0, which adds some new functionality. Backward compatibility means that the Service B v2.0 can still work together with Service A v1.0, and it won't break its functionality. The following are some best practices for maintaining backward compatibility:

- Provide sensible defaults or optional values for new APIs. If that's not possible, create a new resource.
- Never rename existing fields or remove them.
- Never make optional things required.
- Mark old API endpoints as obsolete if not used anymore.

- Test the combination of new and existing service versions by passing old messages between them.

If you intend to support rollback functionality with your services, you will need to think about forward compatibility as well. Forward compatibility means that your service can accept and gracefully handle requests for a later version of itself. The main guideline for ensuring forward compatibility is to ignore any additional fields and don't throw errors.

Semantic Versioning

Using *semantic versioning* is almost a standard by this point. The semantic versioning (*major.minor.patch*) gives guidelines on when to increase which part of the version number:

- Major version is increased when you make API-incompatible changes.
- Minor version is increased when you add backward-compatible features.
- Patch version is increase when you make backward-compatible bug fixes.

You can apply this type of versioning at the API level to communicate to your consumers about the types of changes that were made.

Service Communication

Networking and service communication are essential topics in distributed systems because they can have a significant impact on the overall performance of an application. Therefore, it is beneficial to understand the various service communication options when you are designing and implementing cloud native applications. At a high level, you can differentiate between external service communication and internal service communication. Whereas internal refers to communication within a cluster (i.e., service-to-service communication in the same Kubernetes cluster), external communication refers to communication from or to external services such as Database as a Service (DBaaS) offerings. External service communication from a client into a cluster is often referred to as North-South traffic, and internal service communication is often referred to as East-West traffic. In the context of Kubernetes, ingress controllers are used for North-South and egress controllers can be used to access external services. Kubernetes provides load balancing East-West traffic out of the box by using kube-proxy, but service meshes provide some richer capabilities. Service meshes, ingress, and egress are addressed later in this chapter in "Gateways" on page 55 and "Service Mesh" on page 59.

Protocols

Most of the time, HTTP is used as the protocol for the communication between clients and cloud native applications; however, it is not the most performant of protocols. Large microservices applications can have hundreds or even thousands of services, and the more services you have, the more communication and data exchange need to happen. As a result, the protocol selected becomes an essential factor that can affect performance, and changing communication protocols for productions services can be reasonably expensive. Even though HTTP is a natural choice for communication from a client to your service over the internet, you should consider other protocols for communication between internal services to improve performance. Figure 3-8 shows how you can use a proxy to carry out a protocol transform. We cover this in more detail later in the chapter when we discuss ingress controllers and gateways.

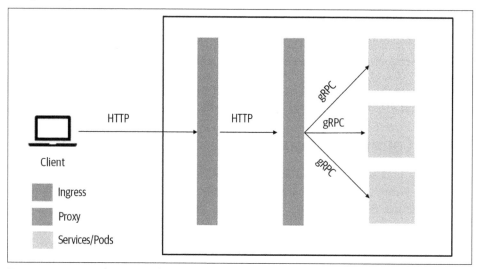

Figure 3-8. Proxy for protocol translation

Next we'll discuss several popular protocols that are proven to provide better performance in cloud native applications.

WebSockets

WebSockets were standardized in 2013 and represent a standard for bidirectional real-time communication between servers and clients. They allow a long-held single TCP socket connection to be established between the client and server, which provides for bidirectional, full-duplex messages to be instantly distributed with little overhead. The WebSockets handshake process starts with the client sending a regular HTTP request to the server. An Upgrade header is included in this request, which informs the server that the client wants to establish a WebSocket connection. When the handshake is complete, the initial HTTP connection is replaced by a WebSocket connection that uses the same underlying TCP/IP connection. WebSockets allow for transferring large data volumes without incurring the overhead associated with traditional HTTP requests. The result is a very low-latency connection.

HTTP/2

HTTP/2 does not entirely replace HTTP. The present verbs, status codes, and most of the headers will remain the same as today. HTTP/2 is primarily designed for low latency, and multiplexing requests over a single TCP connection using streams, improving the efficiency in the way in which data is transferred on the wire. HTTP/2 is a binary protocol, whereas HTTP 1.x is textual. Binary protocols are more efficient to parse because there is only one code path, which makes them very efficient on the wire.

gRPC

gRPC is a fairly new protocol that is quickly gaining in popularity in the microservices community due to its performance and developer friendliness. gRPC is a high-performance, lightweight communication framework using HTTP/2 as the transport protocol, providing features such as authentication, bidirectional streaming and flow control, blocking or nonblocking bindings, and cancellation and timeouts. gRPC uses protocol buffers, aka protobufs, which provide a way of defining and serializing structured data into an efficient binary format. Due to their binary format, they are also small payloads that are quick to send over the wire.

Messaging Protocols

As mentioned earlier, cloud native applications embrace event-driven and message-based approaches, so it is worth mentioning messaging protocols. There are many messaging protocols out there: STOMP, WAMP, AMQP, and MQTT, to name a few. Although describing each protocol is beyond the scope of this book, let's nonetheless take a quick look at the two most popular messaging protocols.

Message Queue Telemetry Transport

The Message Queue Telemetry Transport (MQTT) is a binary protocol that is mainly associated with IoT and machine-to-machine scenarios. It was designed for low-bandwidth environments with unpredictable network connectivity. For instance, MQTT is often used for communication between sensors and gateways. It is a very lightweight protocol that focuses on publisher/subscriber messaging with some additional features such as delivery guarantees. MQTT's strengths are simplicity and a compact binary packet payload.

Advanced Message Queuing Protocol

The Advanced Message Queuing Protocol (AMQP) is a binary protocol that is mainly designed around messaging with a rich feature set, including reliable queuing, topic-based publisher/subscriber, routing, security, and transactions. The rich feature set does not make it a particularly lightweight or fast protocol. That said, AMQP has been battle-tested by various vendors and has been proven to be very reliable. One of the main reasons to use AMQP is its interoperability between different vendors.

Both protocols are used with WebSockets over TCP, which makes them suitable for environments that restrict traffic over port 443 (HTTPS).

A general rule of thumb is to use MQTT if you need simple, reliable messaging, and AMQP if you need to focus on interoperability and functionality that goes beyond simple messaging.

Serialization Considerations

Besides protocols, data serialization and deserialization can affect the overall performance and, in the worst case, become a bottleneck.

JSON is probably the most widely used format right now. JSON is readable, self-contained, and easily extensible, but it has a reasonably large memory footprint, and the serialization and deserialization can be expensive in high data volumes.

Protobuf uses a binary format, and as a result you need a generator for every language, as opposed to JSON, which is just a string format and understood in every modern language. The good news is that there are generators available for pretty much any modern language. With protobufs, the schema is declared in a proto file beforehand, instead of passing the schema with every message like in JSON. The proto file is added to every service that needs to serialize and deserialize the data, and the generator generates an object representing the data; no serialization code is required.

Even though protobufs are probably the way to go when performance matters and you need to deal with a high volume of data, you also can do a couple of things to improve JSON serialization and deserialization:

- Choose a good JSON serializer.
- Consider whether you need to reserialize the object if a downstream service works with the same object. Instead, you can augment the deserialized object and pass it on to another service in a form.

Idempotency

No matter whether you are using synchronous or asynchronous communication, you need to ensure that if the same operation is executed multiple times, the target system remains unchanged. Being able to run an operation multiple times without changing the result is called *idempotency*. As you will see later in the chapter, messages can be received and processed more than once based on failed receivers, retry policies, and so on. Ideally, the receiver should handle the message in an idempotent way so that the repeated call produces the same result.

Let's assume that a wearable device adds some health data to a queue, and a service picks it up to add it to a personal health scorecard. The following message could look similar to the one submitted by the device:

```
{
    "heartrate" : {
    "time" : "20200203073000",
    "bpm" : "89"
    }
}
```

Let's assume further that the operation fails due to some network issues and the receiver cannot pick up the message, so the service sends the message again due to some retry policies. Now you end up with the same message twice. If the receiver now picks up the messages and process them both, the heart rate will be shown as 178 bpm, which probably causes some concern for most people. To avoid this, you need to make the operation idempotent. A common way of ensuring that an operation is idempotent is by adding a unique identifier to the message and making sure that the service processes the message only if the identifiers do not match. The following is an example of the same message, but with an identifier added:

```
{
    "heartrate" : {
    "heartrateID" : "124e456-e89b-12d3-a456-426655440000"
    "time" : "20200203073000",
    "bpm" : "89"
    }
}
```

Now, the receiver can check whether the message has already been processed before processing it. This is also commonly referred to as *de-duping*. The same principle applies to data updates. The bottom line is that you should design operations to be idempotent so that each step can be repeated without affecting the system.

Request/Response

Request/response, also known as request/reply, is a very straightforward message exchange pattern that can be implemented synchronously and asynchronously. The concept is straightforward, as shown in Figure 3-9. Service A requests data from Service B (1), and Service B processes the request and sends the data back to Service A (2).

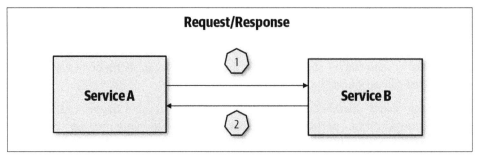

Figure 3-9. Simple request/response

If you use an asynchronous communication pattern you will be facing the issue that both Service A and Service B can engage in multiple communications, so you need to make sure that Service A receives the appropriate response for the request. One way to solve this is by introducing a request and a response queue and using correlation IDs (CIDs), as shown in Figure 3-10.

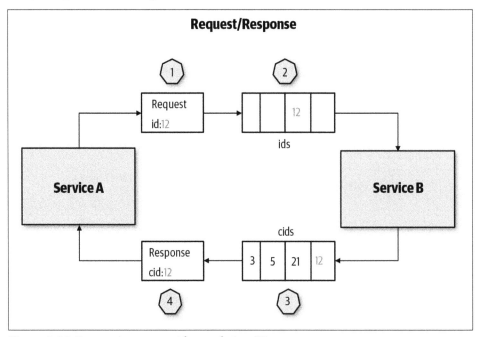

Figure 3-10. Request/response with correlation ID

At a high level, request/response with a CID implements the following steps:

1. Service A creates a request for a record such as a username with an ID, in this case 12, and waits for a message with CID 12 to be returned.

2. Service B picks the message from the queue, retrieves the data for that user, and assigns a CID based on the ID.

3. Service B adds the CID 12 to the response along with the user data and sends the response back. The response queue can have many more responses with CIDs 3,5,21.

4. Service A picks the response with the CID that relates to the request ID.

Publisher/Subscriber

Publisher/subscriber (sub/sub) is one of the most common patterns to facilitate asynchronous communication within a cloud native application. The publisher publishes a message to a topic, which will immediately be picked up by all the subscribers that have subscribed to the topic. Pub/sub serves two main scenarios:

- Enable loose coupling between services and functions because it decouples publishers from subscribers.
- Enable event-driven design, which is a wildly popular design approach for cloud native applications.

At a high level, pub/sub uses the following steps, which are illustrated in Figure 3-11:

1. Service A published a message to a topic.

2. A messaging broker notifies all of the subscribers that are subscribed to that topic.

3. The subscribers consume the message.

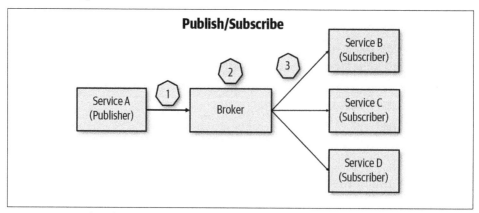

Figure 3-11. Pub/sub architecture

There are a few things you need to keep in mind when using this pattern for dealing with the state:

- By default, the order of messages is not guaranteed, so you need to design for idempotent operations to avoid issues when a message is processed twice.
- Stateful applications, on the other hand, do care about message ordering, so you need to plan for this by taking advantage of the messaging system's built-in ordering functionality or by applying a priority queue pattern.
- If message processing results in an error or even crash of the consumer—for example, due to a faulty format—make sure you do not return the message and instead put it into a poison message queue.

Queues are an essential part of pub/sub messaging; the question, then, is what is the difference between pub/sub and message queues? The key difference is that with message queues each message is processed only once, by a single consumer, as opposed to pub/sub messaging in which multiple receivers subscribed to a topic can consume a message. That said, message queues can support high rates of consumption by adding multiple consumers for each topic, but only one consumer will receive each message on the topic.

Choosing Between Pub/Sub and Request Response

In a cloud native architecture, choosing between pub/sub and request/response really depends on the use case. Figure 3-12 shows the same cloud native application using request/response and pub/sub to highlight some of the differences in a practical example:

1. In the request/response architecture, S1 receives an asynchronous request from a client. After it has processed the request and saved the data, S1 sends a request to S2 and S3.

2. After S3 has processed the request and saved the data, it sends a request to S4 and S5.

3. Now S3 must wait for a response from S4 and S5. If either service fails for some reason S3 waits for it and after a timeout, it will send a timeout to S1, and S1 will send a timeout to the client. For the client, it can be a very long time until it is notified that the request failed. To make matters worse, if the client makes the same request again you can end up with inconsistent data, except that you have made the operation idempotent, as S1 and S3 have already processed the request.

Overall, request/response is making your services tightly coupled, which has all the disadvantages mentioned previously. If you use a pub/sub pattern, on the other hand, you decoupled all of the services, and the communication between the services is handled by passing messages into a pub/sub system such as Redis, RabbitMQ, or Apache Kafka.

1. In the pub/sub architecture, a client sends an asynchronous request to S1. S1 processes the request, saves the data, and places a message into the pub/sub system, and S1 can report back to the client.

2. S2 and S3 have subscribed to the topic in the message broker and can pick up the message.

3. S3 can then process the message and save it and then report back to S2 that the operation was successful. S4 and S5 have subscribed and can pick up the message when ready. The pub system ensures that the message is delivered at some point in time, which means that your data will be *eventually consistent*.

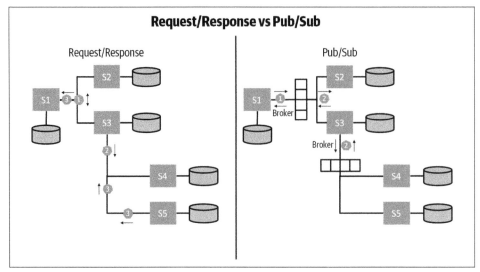

Figure 3-12. Request/response versus pub/sub

Synchronous versus Asynchronous

In a microservices application, each service instance is typically a process. The same is true for using containers with functions. As a result, services and functions must interact using an interprocess communication (IPC) mechanism. You can implement IPC synchronously and asynchronously. Synchronous means that the client waits until a response is available. Synchronous calls are straightforward to understand and to use, so why not implement the entire interservice communication in a synchronous way? There are a few things that you should keep in mind when going down the synchronous path:

Exhaustion of resources
Synchronous means that a thread is blocked while it is waiting for a response. This behavior easily can lead to depletion of resources in a scale scenario.

Response latency
For example, if a user-facing service calls Service A, Service A calls Service B, and so on, the total response time is the sum of the individual service responses. If one service is slow to respond, it holds up the entire response and the application latency increases, which usually results in miserable users.

Cascading failures
Similar to response latencies, a failure in one of the services can lead to a cascading failure that could ultimately lead to a complete breakdown of the application.

Instead of implementing solutions to solve the potential problems that you run into by using synchronous communication, you should consider using asynchronous communication between services. With asynchronous communication between services, the client makes a call but does not block until it gets a response; instead, it can use the freed-up resources to do other things. In a cloud native world, event and queue-based asynchronous messaging are the most popular patterns for IPC.

Gateways

In the world of microservices and functions, the functionality clients require usually spreads across multiple services and functions. How do clients know what endpoints to call? Also, what happens if you redeploy existing services to different endpoints or introduce new services?

At a higher level, you can differentiate between two types of gateways: *API gateways* and *application gateways*. The latter doesn't necessarily have anything to do with the APIs, and they are typically used for Secure Sockets Layer (SSL) offloading and routing for static resources (HTML, CSS files, etc.) or routing to object storage.

The API gateways can help to solve the problems we mentioned earlier. One or more API gateways can sit between the clients and services. Their responsibility can vary—from routing incoming requests to underlying services to exposing business APIs through a common endpoint, and performing tasks such as SSL termination or authentication. Additionality, gateways can be layered: you can have one gateway responsible for offloading SSL, the next one will do the authentication and authorization, and then the last one might do the actual routing to the underlying services.

Routing

Routing is one of the most common functions of a gateway. In this scenario, a gateway acts as a reverse proxy and routes incoming requests to backend services, as shown in Figure 3-13. A reverse proxy typically sits inside a private network and manages incoming client requests to the appropriate backend services.

The pattern is useful when clients need to communicate with one endpoint. The gateway is then responsible for routing the request to the various services based on IP, port, headers, or the URL. This simplifies the logic that clients need to implement because only single endpoints need to be used.

When making decisions on whether to use this pattern, you need to take into account the operating costs and maintaining the gateway. Because you are abstracting multiple services behind one endpoint, the gateway might also become a severe bottleneck; you need to ensure that the gateway can handle the load and scale it appropriately. Alternatively, you can use one of the cloud-provider–managed gateway services and have it take care of operating and maintaining the gateway for you.

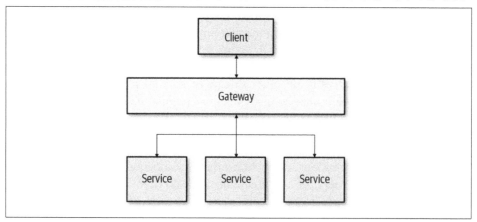

Figure 3-13. Gateway used for routing

Aggregation

A gateway can also act as an aggregator: it takes one request from the client and makes multiple requests to the underlying services. It then aggregates the service responses and returns the single response back to the client, as shown in Figure 3-14.

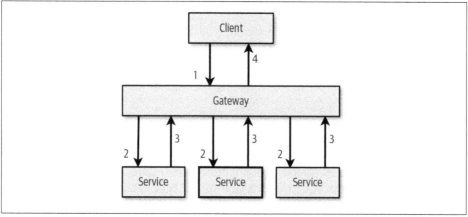

Figure 3-14. Aggregating multiple requests into a single one

When a client makes a request (1), the gateway makes multiple requests to underlying services or functions (2), the services respond (3), and the gateway aggregates the results and returns it to the client (4). The main benefit of this approach is to reduce the traffic between clients and services; instead of a client making multiple requests to different endpoints it creates a single request to the gateway. One thing to note with gateway aggregations is to ensure that you are not introducing any coupling between the gateway and services. If you are doing aggregation in the gateway, be cognizant of the additional load that's being introduced. Also, be careful with adding to the gateway that might cause it to become a monolith. If your aggregation logic is becoming too much for the gateway or if the gateway is breaking down from the load, it might work better if you introduce a separate aggregation or batch service, as shown in Figure 3-15.

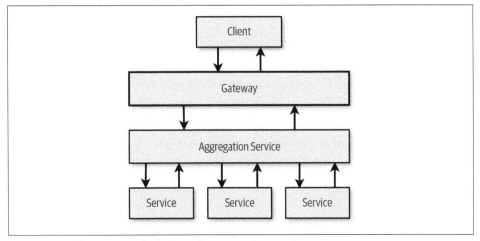

Figure 3-15. Gateway with dedicated aggregation service

Moving the aggregation logic out of the gateway lessens the load on the gateway. It also gives you the ability to separately update the aggregation/batching service, without affecting the gateway.

Offloading

One of the most common uses for gateways is to offload different functionality from individual services and do them at the gateway level. For example, instead of having each service be responsible for SSL termination, you can offload this functionality to the gateway instead. Using SSL termination also separates security assets like certificates.

If you decide to use the offloading, make sure that you are offloading only functionality that's used by all services, often referred to as *cross-cutting concerns*, and never offload any business logic to the gateway. Here are some examples of functionality that can be offloaded from the individual services and used at the gateway level:

- Authentication and authorization
- Rate limiting, retry policies, circuit breaking
- Caching
- Compression

- SSL offloading

- Logging and monitoring

You need to keep in mind that the performance can decrease as you offload more functionality into the gateway. Therefore, just as it is essential to monitor your service, it is essential to monitor the gateways as well.

Implementing Gateways

There are multiple technologies available for implementing gateways. The most popular proxies that are used for gateways are NGINX, HAProxy, and Envoy. All of these are reverse proxies that offer load balancing, SSL, and routing. All these proxies are battle-tested in many production scenarios

In addition to implementing your gateway, you could decide to go the managed route and use one of the cloud providers' offerings, such as Azure Application Gateway, Azure Frontdoor, or Amazon API Gateway.

Egress

The previous section examined ingress gateways that deal with traffic entering your system and can do various tasks such as routing or offloading functionality. Similarly, an *egress gateway* running inside your private network can help direct and control all traffic exiting the private network. This enables your services to access any external services in a controlled way. For example, you can use an egress gateway to block all outbound connections from your private network. This is crucial for security in case your services are compromised. Blocking all outbound connections prevents potential attackers from making outbound calls and perform further attacks.

Using an egress gateway as part of a service mesh such as Istio offers even more granular control over outgoing traffic and provides additional features such as Transport Layer Security (TLS) origination. For example, you can configure Istio to perform TLS origination for traffic to external services where the egress gateway accepts unencrypted internal HTTP connections, encrypt the requests, and forward them to external services. Additionally, you can control the use of wildcard hosts to direct traffic to a set of hosts within a common domain; for example, allowing access to *.example.com, or limit egress traffic to a set of IP addresses.

You should consider using an egress gateway if you need to monitor or control access to external services.

Service Mesh

In the cloud native world, each service is built and deployed independently, and each service potentially communicates with other microservices. As your solution grows, you develop more and more microservices, which also means the communication between services increases and also becomes more complicated. With communication being important, your services need to be resilient and almost immune to any network issues. You need to have a way to implement request retries and define timeouts, circuit breakers, and similar. Having a single library with communication-specific functionality that does all this is one way to go, but it might not help you much if your services are implemented using different programming languages. You could decide to rewrite it for each language separately, but you end up with services using the same functionality but implemented in a different language, as shown in Figure 3-16.

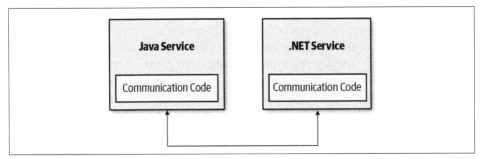

Figure 3-16. Service using separate libraries with the same functionality

Managing libraries can quickly become a nightmare because you need to ensure that each language-specific implementation of the library is up-to-date with the others. Any changes made to one version of the library need to be made to all different versions, and so on.

One of the ideas behind the service mesh is to increase developer productivity by moving common functionality out of each service and into the service mesh. This also allows for the separation of concerns between the service features and service mesh common functionality. If you move the functionality to the mesh, you no longer need to maintain different libraries, and you end up with the state shown in Figure 3-17.

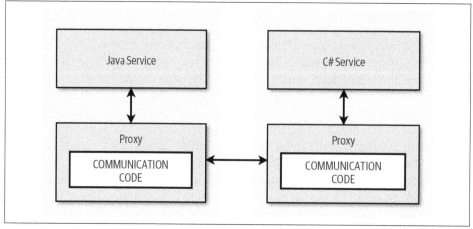

Figure 3-17. Common functionality living inside the proxy

The main building block of any service mesh is a *proxy* that runs next to each service instance. In the case of Kubernetes, the proxy runs as a sidecar in the same pod as your service, and they share the same network. The proxy's job is to intercept all requests entering or exiting the service. Each proxy has its configuration that defines how the incoming or outgoing traffic is handled. In addition to dealing with the traffic and requests, the proxy also emits metrics that can be collected by the service mesh control plane. As an alternative to the sidecar proxy, you can run one proxy per host instead—in Kubernetes you can use a DaemonSet to achieve this.

Using the sidecar proxy is simple and doesn't require a lot of configuration; however, there is an additional resource cost because you are running an extra container within each pod. This can become problematic if you run many instances of your services. You could reduce the costs by running a proxy on each host instead; however, the configuration to set this up might not be straightforward as compared to the sidecar proxy. When deciding whether you should go with the sidecar approach or a per-host approach, consider the following:

- The number of services and sidecar proxies: resource consumption grows as the number of service replicas grows. If you have more than one sidecar proxy per service, the resource consumption increases even faster.

- A language sidecar in which proxies are implemented can add to more resource utilization (e.g., if you are using Java).

- Not all services require a dedicated proxy: consider moving from the sidecar pattern to the per-host pattern and reusing proxy functionality (for example, metrics and log aggregation can be done per-host instead of a per-service with a sidecar proxy).

- The number of requests between service and proxy: requests sent to the sidecar proxy go through fewer steps than requests if you're using a per-host proxy.

The Istio service mesh runs the Envoy proxy next to each instance of the service, whereas the other popular service mesh solution, Linkerd2, uses its ultralight transparent proxy written in Rust, and it allows for running the proxy either as a sidecar or one per host. Consul Connect from HashiCorp also supports Envoy. Table 3-1 compares the different service mesh solutions.

Table 3-1. Comparing service mesh solutions

	Istio	Linkerd2	Consul Connect
Proxy pattern	Sidecar	Sidecar	Sidecar
Supported protocols	HTTP 1.1/HTTP2/gRPC/TCP	HTTP 1.1/HTTP2/gRPC/TCP	TCP
Proxy	Envoy	Native	Pluggable (native or Envoy, NGINX, HAProxy)
Encryption	Yes	Yes (experimental)	Yes
Automatic proxy injection	Yes	Yes	Yes
Traffic control	Yes (label based)	Not yet (Linkerd v1.0 supports it)	Yes (pluggable)
Resiliency (timeouts, retries)	Yes	Yes	Pluggable
Tracing	Jaeger	Not yet	Pluggable
Metrics	Prometheus	Prometheus	Prometheus

To clarify how proxies and different service mesh parts work together, let's take an example of a request retry policy that we want to apply to the services running in the mesh. YAML is usually used to define different rules, such as the request retry policies, of the service mesh. After a rule is applied, the proxies in the service mesh are reconfigured using this rule. The collection of all proxies in the service mesh is usually referred to as the *data plane*. The part of the service mesh that controls the data plane is called a *control plane*. A typical service mesh architecture would look something like the one depicted in Figure 3-18.

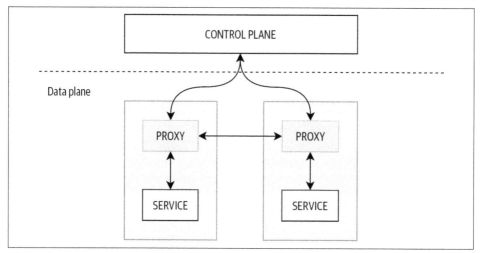

Figure 3-18. Service mesh architecture

As a service mesh user, you don't want to be responsible for managing the proxies in the data plane. One of the control plane's responsibilities is to ensure that the data plane is correctly reconfigured. For example, you want to set the HTTP timeout across your mesh to be 60 seconds. You send a request to the control plane, and the control plane ensures each proxy in the data plane receives a new configuration and reconfigures itself.

The control plane usually exposes an API that is used for configuring the service mesh. In addition to the API, there are generally other services running as part of the control plane; for example, services that handle the policy and telemetry for services running inside the service mesh.

We can group the main features of a service mesh as follows:

- Traffic management
- Failure handling
- Security
- Tracing and monitoring

Traffic management

As the name suggests, the purpose of the traffic management features in the service mesh is to manage traffic between services within the mesh as well as for external services that are being accessed by the in-mesh services.

Each service within a mesh can have multiple endpoint instances. These instances could be VMs, containers, or pods running in Kubernetes. If you are not doing any traffic management, all traffic destined for a service eventually reaches one of the endpoint instances. To manage traffic to the endpoints, you need to define subsets in the pool of all service instances. For example, these instances could be different versions of your service using different Docker images, same-service versions but deployed in different environments, and so on. Figure 3-19 shows an example of different subsets of the same service.

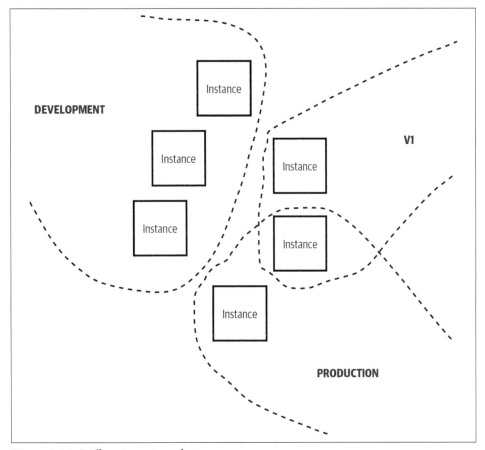

Figure 3-19. Different service subsets

You can use various criteria, such as request headers, URL, or weights associated with specific subsets, to decide which instances receive the incoming traffic. These criteria are usually defined in terms of rules that are sent to the service mesh control plane. The following are some of the most common criteria for traffic routing:

Request headers

You use HTTP headers, URIs scheme, or HTTP methods on the incoming requests to determine whether you want to apply the routing rules. For example, you could route a portion of the traffic to specific subsets only if the request includes a custom header called x-beta-version with a value of 1.

URI

This option uses the request URI to do the matching. You could match parts or full URI to make a decision about where to route the traffic.

Sources

You could route traffic only if it's coming from a specific source. For example, you want to apply rules only if traffic is coming from Service A. If traffic comes from Service B, a different set of routing rules is used.

These rules are applied to the control plane, and the control plane ensures each side-car proxy gets them. Finally, proxies get reconfigured based on these rules and route the traffic accordingly.

Failure handling

In a distributed system you should always assume service communication will fail due to different faults. These faults are not necessarily just because of bugs introduced in the service code. For example, failures can occur due to network or infrastructure issues. There are two types of failures: *transient* and *nontransient*. Transient failures can happen anytime, and most of the time the operation will succeed after a couple of retries. Nontransient failures are more permanent; for example, accessing a file that was deleted. All of this means that you need to write your code in a way that accounts for these types of failures and ensures that your service continues to respond and run correctly.

In addition to the traffic management features, a service mesh should also support how the request failures are handled by defining request timeouts, retries, and circuit breakers. The defaults for timeouts and retries are set per each service and the service version. A service mesh should also have an option of overwriting these settings on a per-request basis, ideally by providing special HTTP headers (Istio, for example, has x-envoy-upstream-rq-timeout-ms and x-envoy-max-retries headers). Keep this in mind when deciding to use these features, because some of the libraries you use could have this functionality included.

Circuit breakers are another feature that you can use to make your services more resilient. The *Circuit Breaker* pattern is used to prevent additional failures and strain on the entire system, by managing access to the failing services. If a circuit breaker trips, it will prevent further access to the failing service.

As part of the Circuit Breaker pattern, you define the conditions or threshold that makes the circuit breaker trip, and you "wrap" your services within the circuit breaker. If the circuit breaker trips based on the set conditions (for example, 10 failures within a 5-second period), the tripped circuit breaker will prevent additional access to the failing service by excluding it.

Circuit breakers need to be defined per each destination that receives the traffic. The implementation of the circuit breaker in the Envoy proxy tracks the status of each host, and if any of the hosts reaches the predefined threshold, it will eject it from the pool of available hosts. If you have 10 instances of your pod running, the circuit breaker will remove any instances that misbehave, so none of the requests can reach them anymore.

In addition to the threshold, you can also define for how long to eject misbehaving hosts (`baseEjectionTime`) as well as the size of the connection pool and the maximum number of requests for each connection.

The other part of failure features is the ability to inject failures into your services. This can significantly help you with testing how the services behave if something goes wrong. There are two ways to inject faults into the services:

HTTP aborts
> This option allows you to abort an incoming request with a specific code. For example, if you ever wondered how your system would behave if a downstream service starts responding with an HTTP 404 error code, you can do this now.

HTTP delays
> In addition to the aborts, you can also test how your service behaves if you inject latency into the request.

Security

At a high level, the security in the service mesh can be broken down to *authentication*, or who you are and what's your identity, and *authorization*, or what can you do or access within the system. The requirements for services security involve traffic encryption for preventing man-in-the-middle attacks and mutual TLS and configurable access policy.

In the Istio service mesh, for example, there are multiple components that work together to deliver the security features for the services running inside the service mesh:

- Citadel provides key and certificate management.
- Envoy proxies running as service sidecars and ingress/egress proxies are responsible for implementing secure communication between services.

- Pilot distributes auth policies and secure naming information to Envoy proxies.
- Mixer manages authorization and auditing.

The relationship between components working together to enable security features is visualized in Figure 3-20.

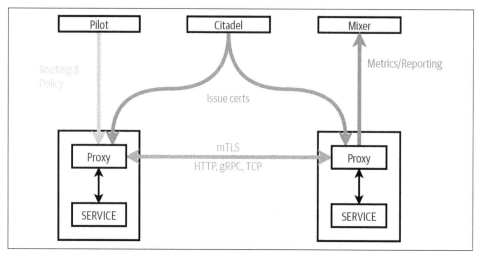

Figure 3-20. Components involved in Istio security

Identity is a fundamental part of any security infrastructure. When two services try to communicate with each other, they need to exchange credentials for mutual authentication purposes. Istio uses the platforms' identity to determine the service identity—for example, for Kubernetes, Istio uses the Kubernetes service accounts. As the next step in the communication between services, the client side checks the servers' identity against the secure naming. The secure naming information is generated automatically and pushed to the sidecar proxies, and it maps the identity to the service name and tells the proxies whether the identity is allowed and authorized to run a service. On the server side, authorization policies are used to determine what information the client can access.

Authentication, mutual TLS, and JWT tokens.   We can differentiate between two types of authentication: *service-to-service authentication* and *end-user authentication.*

You can implement and enable service-to-service or transport authentication by using mutual TLS for each service without making any changes to your services source code. Any requests that service receives will have the authentication policy applied. In Istio, the Citadel is a component that issues the certificates that the proxies use to communicate with one another. The end-user or origin authentication uses JSON web tokens (JWT) to enable request-level authentication.

Any authentication policies defined on the service mesh need to be able to be applied on multiple scopes. With Istio, the policies can be stored in *namespace-scope* or *mesh-scope* storage. The difference between the two is that the policies in the namespace-scope storage affect only services in the same namespaces, and the policies in the mesh-scope affect all services in the mesh. In addition to the scope, each policy needs to specify the services to which the policy applies.

Authorization. You need to define authorization in the service mesh on different levels. Istio, for example, provides the following access control levels:

- Namespace-level access control
- Service-level access control
- Method-level access control

Similarly, as with the authentication policies, Istio stores authorization policies in the config store, and pilot watches for any changes in the policy and updates the proxies. Envoy proxies then evaluate requests against the policies and return the result, ALLOW or DENY.

Authorization can be enabled or disabled with a mesh-wide setting. You can turn the policy on or off for all services, or use inclusion or exclusion settings to either apply the policy to service or except the services from the policy.

Using a separate set of resources, you can define the individual authorization policies for users, groups, or services. The combination of these two resources determines who is allowed to do what under which conditions. For example, you can create an "admin" service role that has access to all services, all methods (GET, POST, PUT, HEAD, etc.), and all paths in the default namespace. Access to services, methods, and paths should also support matching (e.g., apply the role only to paths starting with */api/v1*) because this gives you better control and the ability to come up with more fine-grained rules. For example, you could allow only GET methods on paths that start with API. Additionally, you should also be able to add constraints, which you can use to further constrain the rules based on the destination data (e.g., IP, port, labels, and name) or request headers.

Tracing and monitoring. The fact that all traffic to and from your services in the mesh goes through the proxy allows the service mesh to automatically collect metrics such as the number of requests, their duration, size, response codes, and so on. Collected metrics then are forwarded to another component (Mixer in the case of Istio) where the aggregation happens.

The Mixer component is installed with a built-in Prometheus adapter that exposes an endpoint. Prometheus can then scrape the metrics endpoint on the Mixer to collect the metrics sent from the proxies. Finally, you can visualize the collected metrics by using Grafana, which we explain in more detail in Chapter 5.

Envoy proxies are also configured to send tracing information that can be viewed with Jaeger automatically. As a service developer, you need to ensure that you are attaching trace and span headers to any downstream service requests—this gives Jaeger additional tips on how to tie the traces together.

Each time a request enters the system, the request ID header value is set. This value, (sometimes also referred to as the aforementioned CID) can be used to trace the requests as they make their way through your system. In case of any errors, you could return this ID to the client so that it can be used to trace the failed request and determine what went wrong. Figure 3-21 shows how the request ID is generated and flows through the system.

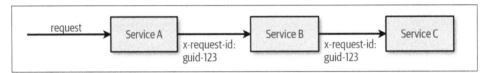

Figure 3-21. Requests with x-request-id header

Example Architecture

An example can go a long way in providing an understanding of concepts such as designing for the cloud. The following example architecture does not cover every scenario, but it does demonstrate how to apply the various concepts. All good architectures are based on business requirements, and the architecturally significant requirements will often be the driving factors in selecting an architectural approach. The architecturally significant requirements will include nonfunctional requirements, which are those that define the quality attributes of the system, like security, scale, performance, availability, and more.

In this example scenario, users are able to manage and view information for multiple types of devices in their home. The service must also be able to support a large and growing number of homes, users, and devices. The device types will continue to grow and the devices within a home will change as users add and change smart devices. The user will be able to manage devices using a mobile application and a single-page application (SPA) from anywhere they can get an internet connection. The user can also receive alerts generated in the device itself or identified in the cloud services. They will also opt in to an agreement allowing the anonymized data from the devices to be analyzed. The service also needs to be able to cater to a growing developer community and home automation hobbyists interested in integrating applications with the cloud services.

The high-level architecture overview presented in Figure 3-22 shows devices connected to a service in the cloud. Devices will be sending large amounts of telemetry data to a service in the cloud at a defined interval and they will receive commands from the cloud that can be generated by users or other events. Users also connect to services in the cloud through a mobile application or a web browser so that they can manage and view information about the devices in their home. Data is analyzed as it's sent to the cloud and is stored for batch analysis. You can read more about data in the cloud in Chapter 4.

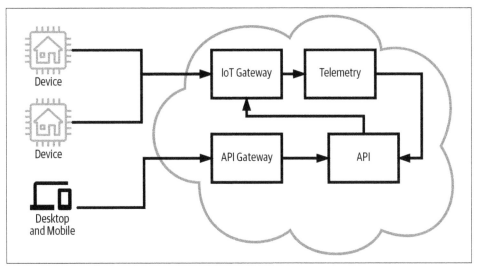

Figure 3-22. High-level example architecture overview

A closer look at the services for storing and analyzing the device telemetry data, as shown in Figure 3-23, shows the data moving through different paths for processing. This split processing of streaming data through hot, warm, and cold paths is also referred to as a *lambda architecture*. You can find more information on storing and analyzing data in Chapter 4. A cloud provider device management service is being used to connect the devices to the cloud. This service could be Azure IoT Hub, AWS IoT Core, or Google Cloud IoT Core.

> Alternatively, devices could connect to a cloud backend through a web API, but this would result in a less optimal service that would then need to be built and operated. This would increase the overall cost of the service and potentially delay the time to market. A cloud native approach uses as much of the cloud.

Devices send their telemetry data through the cloud provider's device management service. The telemetry data is written to a data stream where it can be consumed by multiple different subscribers. Each subscriber is able to work with its own view of the stream processing data at different rates, independent of one another.

As illustrated in Figure 3-23, a cloud provider service is configured to process data from the stream into object storage, which is sometimes referred to as the *cold path*. Object storage is inexpensive, and data for a large number of devices and users can be retained for long periods with minimal infrastructure and operating costs. This data then can be analyzed at a later time, and trends over large periods of time or across a large number of devices can be identified.

Another subscriber processes data into a time-series service, which could be something like Azure Time Series Insights, Amazon Timestream, or even Google BigTable. This data is used for more near-real-time batch analytics and display of device telemetry data over the last hour or days. The data in this service then is automatically moved to slower and cheaper data storage as it ages, and the data is down-sampled because the fidelity of the data over time is less important in this datastore. At some point, the data will expire and is no longer retained in this datastore. Systems needing historical information beyond the defined timeframe will need to load it from cold storage. A process to rehydrate a time-series store from cold storage can be put in place to simplify applications that consume the data.

Another subscriber is processing data from the stream, either performing complex event processing or streaming analytics. This hot path is used to detect conditions in a small period of time from receiving the data. The time can often vary from milliseconds to minutes. This can be used to generate an alert that's sent to the user when temperatures are close to freezing point.

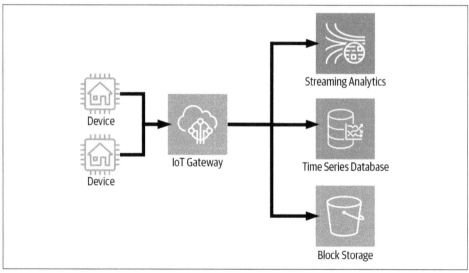

Figure 3-23. Telemetry data ingestion and analytics

The smart home device management service includes a backend API that's used by developers who are interested in integrating with the service, and is used by the clients—both the mobile and the SPA. Figure 3-24 illustrates how the API is composed of multiple services, some of which are containers running in a Kubernetes cluster, and some of which are functions running on the cloud provider's FaaS platform. The team's preferred compute model is FaaS, but some of the workloads are long running or have complex environment requirements, and some teams prefer containers. The various teams are encouraged to use a compute model best suited for their implementation needs. Some of the services use a CaaS compute model through Kubernetes virtual kublet for running some Kubernetes jobs.

An API gateway is used to offload some API management requirements. The API gateway is responsible for authenticating requests and throttling users that are sending an excessive number of requests to maintain quality of service for all users consuming the service.

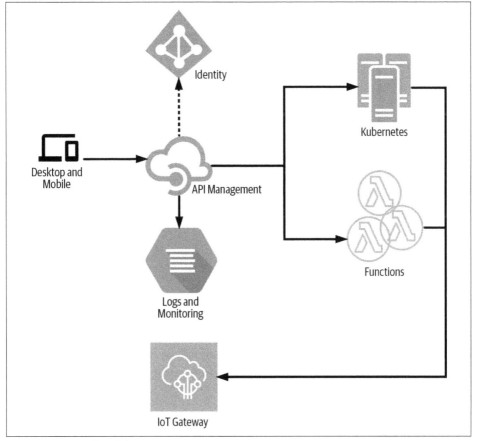

Figure 3-24. Backend device management API

Figure 3-25 shows an SPA being served to a user through a content delivery network (CDN) with a block storage service as the origin. An SPA generally consists of static resources. These static resources can be stored and served to users from block storage. The CDN enables fast loading of these static resources because they are cached at an edge closer to the client. The SPA must make use of cache-busting techniques like putting a hash on resources that have changed, or invalidating specific items in the CDN cache when updates are pushed to storage. The tasks are implemented in the Continuous Delivery pipeline.

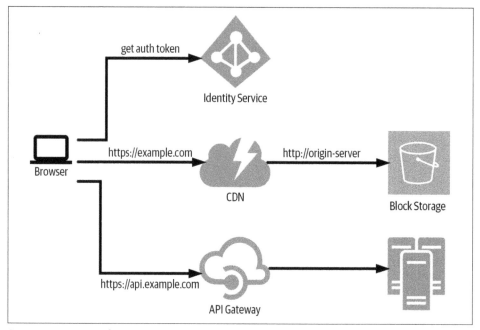

Figure 3-25. Serverless SPA

Summary

As mentioned at the beginning of this chapter, each architecture is different, and there is no one-size-fits-all architecture. Nonetheless, there are specific components and building blocks in a cloud native application architecture that, if designed the wrong way, can cause many problems down the road. By understanding the technologies and patterns described in this chapter, you should be well prepared for designing a cloud native application from the compute side. Chapter 4 covers the other important part of cloud native applications: working with data.

Working with Data

Cloud computing has made a big impact on how we build and operate software today, including how we work with the data. The cost of storing data has significantly decreased, making it cheaper and more feasible for companies to keep vastly larger amounts of data. The operational overhead of database systems is considerably less with the advent of managed and serverless data storage services. This has made it easier to spread data across different data storage types, placing data into the systems better suited to manage the classification of data stored. A trend in microservices architectures encourages the decentralization of data, spreading the data for an application across multiple services, each with its own datastores. It's also common that data is replicated and partitioned in order to scale a system. Figure 4-1 shows how a typical architecture will consist of multiple data storage systems with data spread across them. It's not uncommon that data in one datastore is a copy derived from data in another store, or has some other relationship to data in another store.

Cloud native applications take advantage of managed and serverless data storage and processing services. All of the major public cloud providers offer a number of different managed services to store, process, and analyze data. In addition to cloud provider–managed database offerings, some companies provide managed databases on the cloud provider of your choice. MongoDB, for example, offers a cloud-managed database service called MongoDB Atlas that is available on Amazon Web Services (AWS), Microsoft Azure, and Google Cloud Platform (GCP). By using a managed database, the team can focus on building applications that use the database instead of spending time provisioning and managing the underlying data systems.

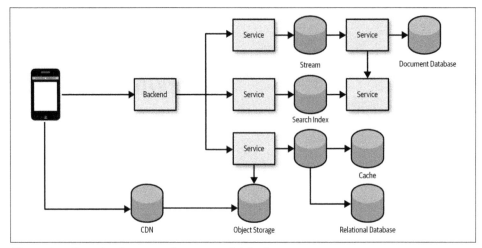

Figure 4-1. Data is often spread across multiple data systems

Serverless database is a term that has been used to refer to a type of managed database with usage-based billing in which customers are charged based on the amount of data stored and processed. This means that if a database is not being accessed, the user is billed only for the amount of data stored. When there is an operation on the database, either the user is charged for the specific operation or the database is scaled from zero and back during the processing of the operation.

Cloud native applications take full advantage of the cloud, including data systems used. The following is a list of cloud native application characteristics for data:

- Prefer managed data storage and analytics services.
- Use polyglot persistence, data partitioning, and caching.
- Embrace eventual consistency and use strong consistency when necessary.
- Prefer cloud native databases that scale out, tolerate faults, and are optimized for cloud storage.
- Deal with data distributed across multiple datastores.

Cloud native applications often need to deal with silos of data, which require a different approach to working with data. There are a number of benefits to polyglot persistence, decentralized data, and data partitioning, but there are also trade-offs and considerations.

Data Storage Systems

There are a growing number of options for storing and processing data. It can be difficult to determine which products to use when building an application. Teams will sometimes engage in a number of iterations evaluating languages, frameworks, and the data storage systems that will be used in the application. Many are still not convinced they made the correct decision, and it's common for those storage systems to be replaced or new ones added as the application evolves anyway.

It can be helpful to understand the various types of datastores and the workloads they are optimized for when deciding which products to use. Many products are, however, multimodel and are designed to support multiple data models, falling into multiple data storage classifications. Applications will often take advantage of multiple data storage systems, storing files in an object store, writing data to a relational database, and caching with an in-memory key/value store.

Objects, Files, and Disks

Every public cloud provider offers an inexpensive *object storage service*. Object storage services manage data as objects. Objects are usually stored with metadata for the object and a key that's used as a reference for the object. File storage services generally provide shared access to files through a traditional file sharing model with a hierarchical directory structure. Disks or block storage provides storage of disk volumes used by computing instances. Determining where to store files such as images, documents, content, and genomics data files will largely depend on the systems that access them. Each of the following storage types is better suited for different types of files:

You should prefer object storage for storing file data. Object storage is relatively inexpensive, extremely durable, and highly available. All of the major cloud providers offer different storage tiers enabling cost saving based on data access requirements.

Object/blob storage
- Use it with files when the applications accessing the data support the cloud provider API.
- It is inexpensive and can store large amounts of data.
- Applications need to implement a cloud provider API. If application portability is a requirement, see Chapter 7.

File storage
- Use it with applications designed to support Network Attached Storage (NAS).
- Use it when using a library or service that requires shared access to files.
- It is more expensive than object storage.

Disk (block) storage
- Use it for applications that assume persistent local storage disks, like MongoDB or a MySQL database.

In addition to the various cloud provider–managed storage options for files and objects, you can provision a distributed filesystem. The Hadoop Distributed File System (HDFS) is popular for big data analytics. The distributed filesystem can use the cloud provider disk or block storage services. Many of the cloud providers have managed services for popular distributed filesystems that include the analytics tools used. You should consider these filesystems when using the analytics tools that work with them.

Databases

Databases are generally used for storing more structured data with well-defined formats. A number of databases have been released over the past few years, and the number of databases available for us to choose from continues to grow every year. Many of these databases have been designed for specific types of data models and workloads. Some of them support multiple models and are often labeled as *multimodel databases*. It helps to organize databases into a group or classification when considering which database to use where in an application.

Key/value

Often, application data needs to be retrieved using only the primary key, or maybe even part of the key. A key/value store can be viewed as simply a very large hash table that stores some value under a unique key. The value can be retrieved very efficiently using the key or, in some cases, part of the key. Because the value is opaque to the database, a consumer would need to scan record-by-record in order to find an item based on the value. The keys in a key/value database can comprise multiple elements and even can be ordered for efficient lookup. Some of the key/value databases allow for the lookup using the key prefix, making it possible to use compound keys. If the data can be queried based on some simple nesting of keys, this might be a suitable option. If we're storing orders for customer xyz in a key/value store, we might store them using the customer ID as a key prefix followed by the order number, "xyz-1001." A specific order can be retrieved using the entire key, and orders for customer xyz could be retrieved using the "xyz" prefix.

Key/value databases are generally inexpensive and very scalable datastores. Key/value data storage services are capable of partitioning and even repartitioning data based on the key. Selecting a key is important when using these datastores because it will have a significant impact on the scale and the performance of data storage reads and writes.

Document

A document database is similar to a key/value database in that it stores a document (value) by a primary key. Unlike a key/value database, which can store just about any value, the documents in a document database need to conform to some defined structure. This enables features like the maintenance of secondary indexes and the ability to query data based on the document. The values commonly stored in a document database are a composition of hashmaps (JSON objects) and lists (JSON arrays). JSON is a popular format used in document databases, although many database engines use a more efficient internal storage format like MongoDB's BSON.

You will need to think differently about how you organize data in a document-oriented database when coming from relational databases. It takes time for many to make the transition to this different approach to data modeling.

You can use these databases for much of what was traditionally stored in a relational database like PostgreSQL. They have been growing in popularity and unlike wwith relational databases, the documents map nicely to objects in programming languages and don't require object relational mapping (ORM) tools. These databases generally don't enforce a schema, which has some advantages with regard to Continuous Delivery (CD) of software changes requiring data schema changes.

Databases that do not enforce a schema are often referred to "schema on read" because although the database does not enforce the schema, an inherent schema exists in the applications consuming the data and will need to know how to work with the data returned.

Relational

Relational databases organize data into two-dimensional structures called tables, consisting of columns and rows. Data in one table can have a relationship to data in another table, which the database system can enforce. Relational databases generally enforce a strict schema, also referred to *schema on write*, in which a consumer writing data to a database must conform to a schema defined in the database.

Relational databases have been around for a long time and a lot of developers have experience working with them. The most popular and commonly used databases, as of today, are still relational databases. These databases are very mature, they're good with data that contains a large number of relationships, and there's a large ecosystem of tools and applications that know how to work with them. *Many-to-many relationships* can be difficult to work with in document databases, but in relational database they are very simple. If the application data has a lot of relationships, especially those that require transactions, these databases might be a good fit.

Graph

A graph database stores two types of information: *edges* and *nodes*. Edges define the relationships between nodes, and you can think of a node as the entity. Both nodes and edges can have properties providing information about that specific edge or node. An edge will often define the direction or nature of a relationship. Graph databases work well at analyzing the relationships between entities. Graph data can be stored in any of the other databases, but when graph traversal becomes increasingly complex, it can be challenging to meet the performance and scale requirements of graph data in the other storage types.

Column family

A column-family database organizes data into rows and columns, and can initially appear very similar to a relational database. You can think of a column-family database as holding tabular data with rows and columns, but the columns are divided into groups known as column families. Each column family holds a set of columns that are logically related together and are typically retrieved or manipulated as a unit. Other data that is accessed separately can be stored in separate column families. Within a column family, new columns can be added dynamically, and rows can be sparse (that is, a row doesn't need to have a value for every column).

Time-series

Time-series data is a database that's optimized for time, storing values based on time. These databases generally need to support a very high number of writes. They are commonly used to collect large amounts of data in real time from a large number of sources. Updates to the data are rare and deletes are often completed in bulk. The records written to a time-series database are usually very small, but there are often a large number of records. Time-series databases are good for storing telemetry data. Popular uses include Internet of Things (IoT) sensors or application/system counters. Time-series databases will often include features for data retention, down-sampling, and storing data in different mediums depending on configuration data usage patterns.

Search

Search engine databases are often used to search for information held in other data-stores and services. A search engine database can index large volumes of data with near-real-time access to the indexes. In addition to searching across unstructured data like that in a web page, many applications use them to provide structured and ad hoc search features on top of data in another database. Some databases have full-text indexing features, but search databases are also capable of reducing words to their root forms through stemming and normalization.

Streams and Queues

Streams and queues are data storage systems that store events and messages. Although they are sometimes used for the same purpose, they are very different types of systems. In an event stream, data is stored as an immutable stream of events. A consumer is able to read events in the stream at a specific location but is unable to modify the events or the stream. You cannot remove or delete individual events from the stream. Messaging queues or topics will store messages that can be changed (mutated), and it's possible to remove an individual message from a queue. Streams are great at recording a series of events, and streaming systems are generally able to store and process very large amounts of data. Queues or topics are great for messaging between different services, and these systems are generally designed for the short-term storage of messages that can be changed and randomly deleted. This chapter focuses more on streams because they are more commonly used with data systems, and queues more commonly used for service communications. For more information on queues, see Chapter 3.

A topic is a concept used in a publish-subscribe messaging model. The only difference between a topic and a queue is that a message on a queue goes to one subscriber, whereas a message to a topic will go to multiple subscribers. You can think of a queue as a topic with one, and only one, subscriber.

Blockchain

Records on a blockchain are stored in a way that they are immutable. Records are grouped in a *block*, each of which contains some number of records in the database. Every time new records are created, they are grouped into a single block and added to the chain. Blocks are chained together using hashing to ensure that they are not tampered with. The slightest change to the data in a block will change the hash. The hash from each block is stored at the beginning of the next block, ensuring that nobody can change or remove a block from the chain. Although a blockchain could be used like any other centralized database, it's commonly decentralized, removing power from a central organization.

Selecting a Datastore

When selecting a datastore, you need to consider a number of requirements. Selecting data storage technologies and services can be quite challenging, especially given the cool new databases constantly becoming available and changes in how we build software. Start with the architecturally significant requirements—also known as *non-functional* requirements—for a system and then move to the functional requirements.

Selecting the appropriate datastore for your requirements can be an important design decision. There are literally hundreds of implementations to choose from among SQL and NoSQL databases. Datastores are often categorized by how they structure data and the types of operations they support. A good place to begin is by considering which storage model is best suited for the requirements. Then, consider a particular datastore within that category, based on factors such as feature set, cost, and ease of management.

Gather as much of the following information as you can about your data requirements.

Functional requirements

Data format
> What type of data do you need to store?

Read and write
> How will the data need to be consumed and written?

Data size
> How large are the items that will be placed in the datastore?

Scale and structure
> How much storage capacity do you need, and do you anticipate needing to partition your data?

Data relationships
> Will your data need to support complex relationships?

Consistency model
> Will you require strong consistency or is eventual consistency acceptable?

Schema flexibility
> What kind of schemas will you apply to your data? Is a fixed or strongly enforced schema important?

Concurrency
> Will the application benefit from multiversion concurrency control? Do you require pessimistic and/or optimistic concurrency control?

Data movement
> Will your application need to move data to other stores or data warehouses?

Data life cycle
> Is the data write-once, read-many? Can it be archived over time or can the fidelity of the data be reduced through down-sampling?

Change streams
> Do you need to support change data capture (CDC) and fire events when data changes?

Other supported features
> Do you need any other specific features, full-text search, indexing, and so on?

Nonfunctional requirements

Team experience
> Probably one of the biggest reasons teams select a specific database solution is because of experience.

Support
> Sometimes the database system that's the best technical fit for an application is not the best fit for a project because of the support options available. Consider whether or not available support options meet the organizations needs.

Performance and scalability
> What are your performance requirements? Is the workload heavy on ingestion? Query and analytics?

Reliability
> What are the availability requirements? What backup and restore features are necessary?

Replication
> Will data need to be replicated across multiple regions or zones?

Limits
> Are there any hard limits on size and scale?

Portability
> Do you need to deploy on-premises or to multiple cloud providers?

Management and cost

Managed service
> When possible, use a managed data service. There are, however, situations for which a feature is not available and needed.

Region or cloud provider availability
  Is there a managed data storage solution available?

Licensing
  Are there any restrictions on licensing types in the organization? Do you have a preference of a proprietary versus open source software (OSS) license?

Overall cost
  What is the overall cost of using the service within your solution? A good reason to prefer managed services is for the reduced operational cost.

Selecting a database can be a bit daunting when you're looking across the vast number of databases available today and the new ones constantly introduced in the market. A site that tracks database popularity, db-engines (*https://db-engines.com*), lists 329 different databases as of this writing. In many cases the skillset of the team is a major driving factor when selecting a database. Managing data systems can add significant operational overhead and burden to the team and managed data systems are often preferred for cloud-native applications, so the availability of managed data systems will quite often narrow down the options. Deploying a simple database can be easy, but consider that the patching, upgrades, performance tuning, backups, and highly available database configurations increase operations burden. Yet there are situations in which managing a database is necessary, and you might prefer some of the new databases built for the cloud, like CockroachDB or YugaByte. Also consider available tooling: it might make sense to deploy and manage a certain database if this avoids the need to build software to consume the data, like a dashboard or reporting systems.

Data in Multiple Datastores

Whether you're working with data across partitions, databases, or services, data in multiple datastores can introduce some data management challenges. Traditional transaction management might not be possible and distributed transactions will adversely affect the performance and scale of a system. The following are some of the challenges of distributing data:

- Data consistency across the datastores
- Analysis of data in multiple datastores
- Backup and restore of the datastores

The consistency and integrity of the data can be challenging when spread across multiple datastores. How do you ensure a related record in one system is updated to reflect a change in another system? How do you manage copies of data, whether they are cached in memory, a materialized view, or stored in the systems of another service team? How do you effectively analyze data that's stored across multiple silos? Much of this is addressed through data movement, and a growing number of technologies and services are showing up in the market to handle this.

Change Data Capture

Many of the database options available today offer a stream of data change events (change log) and expose this through an easy-to-consume API. This can make it possible to perform some actions on the events, like triggering a function when a document changes or updating a materialized view. For example, successfully adding a document that contains an order could trigger an event to update reporting totals and notify an accounting service that an order for the customer has been created. Given a move to polyglot persistence and decentralized datastores, these event streams are incredibly helpful in maintaining consistency across these silos of data. Some common use cases for CDC include:

Notifications
> In a microservices architecture, it's not uncommon that another service will want to be notified of changes to data in a service. For this, you can use a webhook or subscription to publish events for other services.

Materialized views
> Materialized views make for efficient and simplified queries on a system. The change events can be used to update these views.

Cache invalidation
> Caches are great for improving the scale and performance of a system, but invalidating the cache when the backing data has changed is a challenge. Instead of using a time-to-live (TTL), you can use change events to either remove the cached item or update it.

Auditing
> Many systems need to maintain a record of changes to data. You can use this log of changes to track what was changed and when. The user that made the change is often needed, so it might be necessary to ensure that this information is also captured.

Search
> Many databases are not very good at handling search, and the search datastores do not provide all of the features needed in other databases. You can use change streams to maintain a search index.

Analytics

The data analytics requirements of an organization often require a view across many different databases. Moving the data to a central data lake, warehouse, or database can enable richer reporting and analytics requirements.

Change analytics

Near-real-time analysis of data changes can be separated from the data access concerns and performed on the data changes.

Archive

In some applications, it is necessary to maintain an archive of state. This archive is rarely accessed, and it's often better to store this in a less expensive storage system.

Legacy systems

Replacing a legacy system will sometimes require data to be maintained in multiple locations. These change streams can be used to update data in a legacy system.

In Figure 4-2, we see an app writing to a database that logs a change. That change is then written to a stream of change logs and processed by multiple consumers. Many database systems maintain an internal log of changes that can be subscribed to with checkpoints to resume at a specific location. MongoDB, for example, allows you to subscribe to events on a deployment, data, or collection, and provide a token to resume at a specific location. Many of the cloud provider databases handle the watch process and will invoke a serverless function for every change.

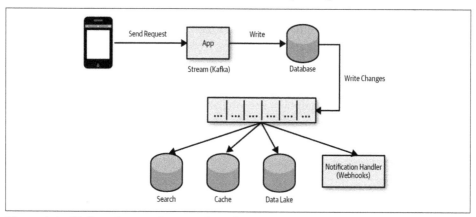

Figure 4-2. CDC used to synchronize data changes

The application could have written the change to the stream and the database, but this presents some problems if one of the two operations fails and it potentially creates a race condition. For example, if the application were updating some data in the database, like an account shipping preference, and then failed to write to an event stream, the data in the database would have changed, but the other systems would not have been notified or updated, like a shipping service. The other concern is that if two processes made a change to the same record at close to the same time, the order to events can be a problem. Depending on the change and how it's processed, this might not be an issue, but it's something to consider. The concern is that we either record the event that something changed when it didn't, or change something and don't record the event.

By using the databases change stream, we can write the change or mutation of the document and the log of that change as a transaction. Even though data systems consuming the event stream are eventually consistent after some period of time, it's important that they become consistent. Figure 4-3 shows a document that has been updated and the change recorded as part of a transaction. This ensures that the change event and the actual change itself are consistent, so now we just need to consume and process that event into other systems.

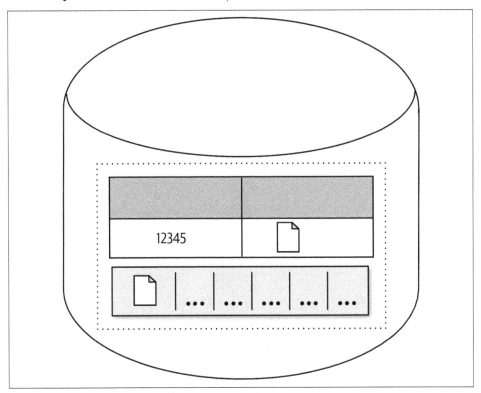

Figure 4-3. Changes to a record and operation log in a transaction scope

Many of the managed data services make this really easy to implement and can be quickly configured to invoke a serverless function when a change happens in the datastore. You can configure MongoDB Atlas to invoke a function in the MongoDB Stitch service. A change in Amazon DynamoDB or Amazon Simple Storage Service (Amazon S3) can trigger a lambda function. Microsoft Azure Functions can be invoked when a change happens in Azure Cosmos DB or Azure Blob Storage. A change in Google Cloud Firestore or object storage service can trigger a Cloud Function. Implementation with popular managed data storage services can be fairly straightforward. This is becoming a popular and necessary feature with most datastores.

Write Changes as an Event to a Change Log

As we just saw an application failure during an operation that affects multiple datastores can result in data consistency issues. Another approach that you can use when an operation spans multiple databases is to write the set of changes to a change log and then apply those changes. A group of changes can be written to a stream maintaining order, and if a failure occurs while the changes are being applied, it can be easy to retry or resume the operation, as shown in Figure 4-4.

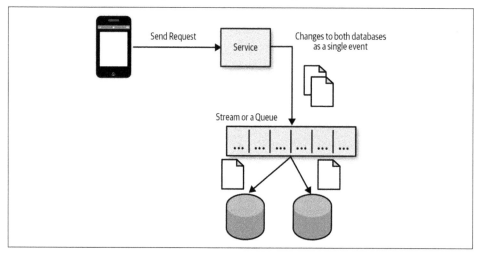

Figure 4-4. Saving a set of changes before writing each change

Transaction Supervisor

You can use a supervisor service to ensure that a transaction is successfully completed or is compensated. This can be especially useful when you're performing transactions involving external services—for example, writing an order to the system and processing a credit card, in which credit card processing can fail, or saving the results of the processing. As Figure 4-5 illustrates, a checkout service receives an order, processes a credit card payment, and then fails to save the order to the order database. Most customers would be upset to know that their credit card was processed but there was no record of their order. This is a fairly common implementation.

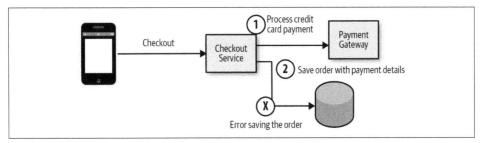

Figure 4-5. Failing to save order details after processing an order

Another approach might be to save the order or cart with a status of processing, then make the call to the payment gateway to process the credit card payment, and finally, update the status of the order. Figure 4-6 demonstrates how if we fail to update the order status, at least we have the record of an order submitted and the intention to process it. If the payment gateway service offered a notification service like a webhook callback, we could configure that to ensure that the status was accurate.

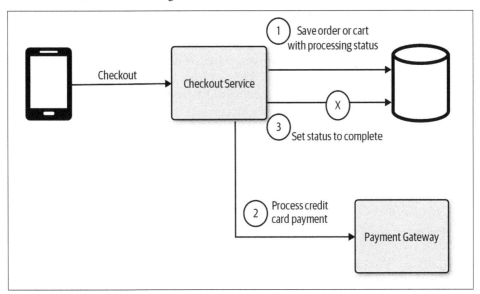

Figure 4-6. Failing to update order status

In Figure 4-7, a supervisor is added to monitor the order database for processing transactions that have not completed and reconciles the state. The supervisor could be a simple function that's triggered at a specific interval.

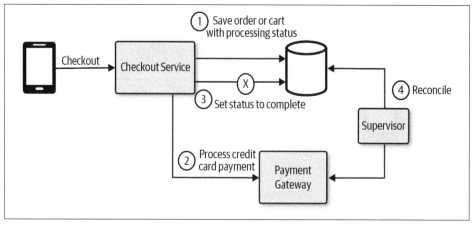

Figure 4-7. A supervisor service monitors transactions for errors

You can use this approach—using a supervisor and setting status—in many different ways to monitor systems and databases for consistency and take action to correct them or generate a notification of the issue.

Compensating Transactions

Traditional distributed transactions are not commonly used in today's cloud native applications, and not always available. There are situations for which transactions are necessary to maintain consistency across services or datastores. For example, a consumer posts some data with a file to an API requiring the application to write the file to object storage and some data to a document database. If we write the file to object storage and then fail when writing to the database, for any reason, we have a potentially orphaned file in object storage if the only way to find it is through a query on the database and reference. This is a situation in which we want to treat writing the file and the database record as a transaction; if one fails, both should fail. The file then should be removed to compensate for the failed database write. This is essentially what a compensating transaction does. A logical set of operations need to complete; if one of the operations fails, we might need to compensate the ones that succeeded.

You should avoid service coordination. In many cases, you can avoid complex transaction coordination by designing for eventual consistency and using techniques like CDC.

Extract, Transform, and Load

The need to move and transform data for business intelligence (BI) is quite common. Businesses have been using Extract, Transform, and Load (ETL) platforms for a long time to move data from one system to another. Data analytics is becoming an important part of every business, large and small, so it should be no surprise that ETL platforms have become increasingly important. Data has become spread out across more systems and analytics tools have become much more accessible. Everyone can take advantage of data analytics, and there's a growing need to move the data into a location for performing data analysis, like a data lake or date warehouse. You can use ETL to get the data from these operational data systems into a system to be analyzed. ETL is a process that comprises the following three different stages:

Extract

> Data is extracted or exported from business systems and data storage systems, legacy systems, operational databases, external services, and event Enterprise Resource Planning (ERP) or Customer Relationship Management (CRM) systems. When extracting data from the various sources, it's important to determine the velocity, how often the data is extracted from each source, and the priority across the various sources.

Transform

> Next, the extracted data is transformed; this would typically involve a number of data cleansing, transformation, and enrichment tasks. The data can be processed off a stream and is often stored in an interim staging store for batch processing.

Load

> The transformed data then is loaded into the destination and can be analyzed for BI.

All of the major cloud providers offer managed ETL services, like AWS Glue, Azure Data Factory, and Google Cloud DataFlow. Moving and processing data from one source to another is increasingly important and common in today's cloud native applications.

Microservices and Data Lakes

One challenge of dealing with decentralized data in a microservices architecture is the need to perform reporting or analysis across data in multiple services. Some reporting and analytics requirements will need the data from the services to be in a common datastore.

It might not be necessary to move the data in order to perform the required analysis and reporting across all of the data. Some or all of the analysis can be performed on each of the individual datastores in conjunction with some centralized analysis tasks on the results.

Having each service work from a shared or common database will, however, violate one of the microservices principles and potentially introduce coupling between the services. A common way to approach this is through data movement and aggregating the data into a location for a reporting or analytics team. In Figure 4-8, data from multiple microservices datastores is aggregated into a centralized database in order to deliver the necessary reporting and analytics requirements.

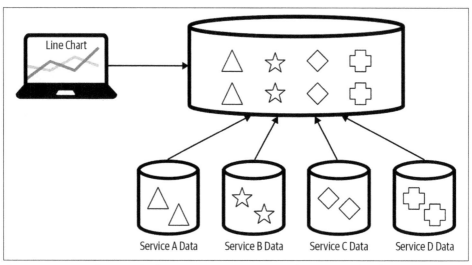

Figure 4-8. Data from multiple microservices aggregated in a centralized datastore

The data analytics or reporting team will need to determine how to get the data from the various service teams that it requires for the purpose of reporting without introducing coupling. There are a number of ways to approach this, and it will be important to ensure loose coupling is maintained, allowing the teams to remain agile and deliver value quickly.

The individual services team could give the data analytics teams read access to the database and allow them to replicate the data, as depicted in Figure 4-9. This would be a very quick and easy approach, but the service team does not control when or how much load the data extraction will put on the store, causing potential performance issues. This also introduces coupling, and it's likely that the service teams then will need to coordinate with the data analytics team when making internal schema changes. The ETL load on the database adversely affecting service performance can be addressed by giving the data analytics team access to a read replica instead of the primary data. It might also be possible to give the data analytics team access to a view on the data instead of the raw documents or tables. This would help to mitigate some of the coupling concerns.

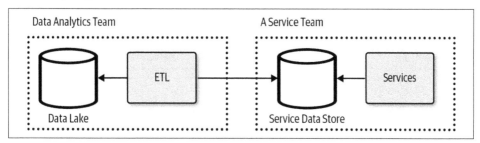

Figure 4-9. The data analytics team consumes data directly from the service team's database

This approach can work in the early phases of the application with a handful of services, but it will be challenging as the application and teams grow. Another approach is to use an *integration datastore*. The service team provisions and maintains a datastore for internal integrations, as shown in Figure 4-10. This allows the service team to control what data and the shape of the data in the integration repository. This integration repository should be managed like an API, documented and versioned. The service team could run ETL jobs to maintain the database or use CDC and treat it like a materialized view. The service team could make changes to its operational store without affecting the other teams. The service team would be responsible for the integration store.

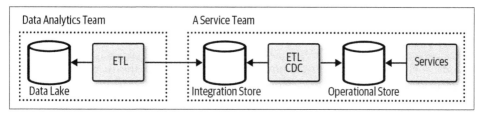

Figure 4-10. Database as an API

This could be turned around such that a service consumer, like the data analytics team, asks a service team to export or write data to the data lake, as illustrated in Figure 4-11, or to a staging store, as in Figure 4-12. The service teams support replication or data, logs, or data exports to a client-provided location as part of the service features and API. The data analytics team would provision a store or location in a datastore for each service team. The data analytics team then subscribes to data needed for aggregated analytics.

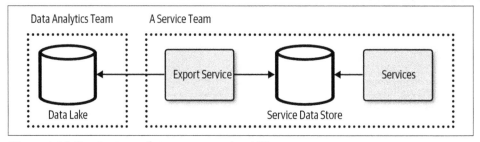

Figure 4-11. Service team data export service API

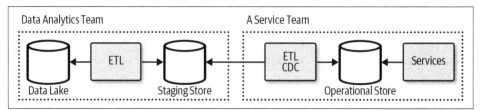

Figure 4-12. Service teams write to a staging store

It's not uncommon for services to support data exports. The service implementation would define what export format and protocols are part of its API. This, for example, would be a configuration for an object storage location and credentials to which to send nightly exports, or maybe a webhook to which to send batches of changes. A service consumer such as the data analytics team would have access to the service API, allowing it to subscribe to data changes or exports. The team could send locations and credentials to which to either dump export files or send events.

Client Access to Data

Clients applications generally do not have direct access to the datastores in most applications built today. Data is commonly accessed through a service that's responsible for performing authorizations, auditing, validation, and transformation of the data. The service is usually responsible for carrying out other functions, although in many data-centric applications, a large part of the service implementation simply handles data read and write operations.

A simple data-centric application would generally require you to build and operate a service that performs authentication, authorization, logging, transformations, and validation of data. It does, however, need to control who can access what within the datastore and validate what's being written. Figure 4-13 shows a typical frontend application calling a backend service that reads and writes to a single database. This is a common architecture for many applications today.

Figure 4-13. Client application with a backend service and database

Restricted Client Tokens (Valet-Key)

A service can create and return a token to a consumer that has limited use. This can actually be implemented using OAuth or even a custom cryptographically signed policy. The valet key is commonly used as a metaphor to explain how OAuth works and is a commonly used cloud design pattern. The token returned might be able to access only a specific data item for a limited period of time or upload a file to a specific location in a datastore. This can be a convenient way to offload processing from a service, reducing the cost and scale of the service and delivering better performance. In Figure 4-14, a file is uploaded to a service that writes the file to storage.

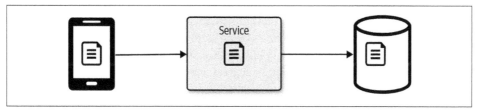

Figure 4-14. Client uploading a file that's passed through the service

Instead of streaming a file through the service, it can be much more efficient to return a token to the client with a location to access the file if it were reading or uploading the file to a specific location. In Figure 4-15, the client requests a token and a location from the service, which then generates a token with some policies. The token policy can restrict the location to which the file can be uploaded, and it's a best practice to set an expiration so that the token cannot be used anytime later on. The token should follow the principle of *least privilege*, granting the minimum permissions necessary to complete the task. In Microsoft Azure Blob Storage, the token is also referred to as a *shared-access signature*, and in Amazon S3, this would be a *presigned URL*. After the file is uploaded, an object storage function could be used to update the application state.

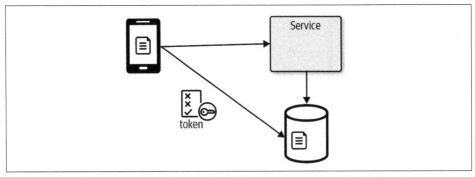

Figure 4-15. The client gets a token and path from a service to upload directly to storage

Database Services with Fine-Grained Access Control

Some databases provide fine-grained access control to data in the database. These database services are sometimes called a Backend as a Service (BaaS) or Mobile Backend as a Service (MBaaS). A full-featured MBaaS will generally offer more than just data storage, given that mobile applications often need identity management and notification services as well. This almost feels like we have circled back to the days of the old thick-client applications. Thankfully, data storage services have evolved so that it's not exactly the same. Figure 4-16 presents a mobile client connecting to a database service without having to deploy and manage an additional API. If there's no need to ship a customer API, this can be a great way to quickly get an application out with low operational overhead. Careful attention is needed with releasing updates and testing the security rules to ensure that only the appropriate people are able to access the data.

Figure 4-16. A mobile application connecting to a database

Databases such as Google's Cloud FireStore allow you to apply security rules that provide access control and data validation. Instead of building a service to control access and validate requests, you write security rules and validation. A user is required to authenticate to Google Firebase Authentication service, which can federate to other identity providers, like Microsoft's Azure Active Directory services. After a user is authenticated, the client application can connect directly to the database service and read or write data, provided the operations satisfy the defined security rules.

GraphQL Data Service

Instead of building and operating a custom service to manage client access to data, you can deploy and configure a GraphQL server to provide clients access to data. In Figure 4-17, a GraphQL service is deployed and configured to handle authorization, validation, caching, and pagination of data. Fully managed GraphQL services, like AWS AppSync, make it extremely easy to deploy a GraphQL-based backend for your client services.

> GraphQL is neither a database query language nor storage model; it's an API that returns application data based on a schema that's completely independent of how the data is stored.

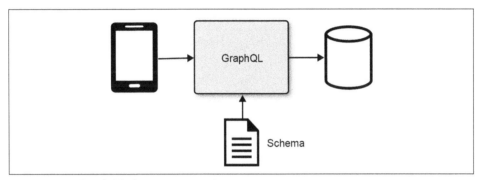

Figure 4-17. GraphQL data access service

GraphQL is flexible and configurable through a GraphQL specification. You can configure it with multiple providers, and even configure it to execute services either running in a container or deployed as functions that are invoked on request, as shown in Figure 4-18. GraphQL is a great fit for data-centric backends with the occasional service method that needs to be invoked. Services like GitHub are actually moving their entire API over to GraphQL because this provides more flexibility to the consumers of the API. GraphQL can be helpful in addressing the over-fetching and chattiness that's sometimes common with REST-based APIs.

GraphQL uses a schema-first approach, defining nodes (objects) and edges (relationships) as part of a schema definition for the graph structure. Consumers can query the schema for details about the types and relationships across the objects. One benefit of GraphQL is that it makes it easy to define the data you want, and only the data you want, without having to make multiple calls or fetch data that's not needed. The specification supports authorizations, pagination, caching, and more. This can make it quick and easy to create a backend that handles most of the features needed in a data-centric application. For more information, visit the GraphQL website (*http://www.graphql.org*).

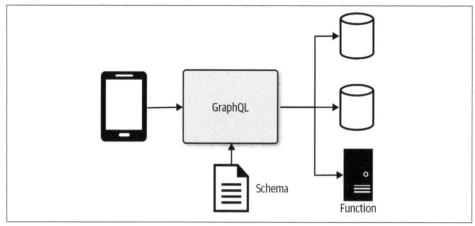

Figure 4-18. GraphQL service with multiple providers and execution

Fast Scalable Data

A large majority of application scaling and performance problems can be attributed to the databases. This is a common point of contention that can be challenging to scale out while meeting an application's data-quality requirements. In the past, it was too easy to put logic into a database in the form of stored procedures and triggers, increasing compute requirements on a system that was notoriously expensive to scale. We learned to do more in the application and rely less on the database for something other than focusing on storing data.

 There are very few reasons to put logic in a database. Don't do it. If you go there, make sure that you understand the trade-offs. It might make sense in a few cases and it might improve performance, but likely at the cost of scalability.

Scaling anything and everything can be achieved through replication and partitioning. Replicating the data to a cache, materialized view, or read-replica can help increase the scalability, availability, and performance of data systems. Partitioning data either horizontally through sharding, vertically based on data model, or functionally based on features will help improve scalability by distributing the load across systems.

Sharding Data

Sharding data is about dividing the datastore into horizontal partitions, known as *shards*. Each shard contains the same schema, but holds a subset of the data. Sharding often is used to scale a system by distributing the load across multiple data storage systems.

When sharding data, it's important to determine how many shards to use and how to distribute the data across the shards. Deciding how to distribute the data across shards heavily depends on the application's data. It's important to distribute the data in such a way that one single shard does not become overloaded and receive all or most of the load. Because the data for each shard or partition is commonly in a separate datastore, it's important that the application can connect to the appropriate shard (partition or database).

Caching Data

Data caching is important to scaling applications and improving performance. Caching is really just about copying the data to a faster storage medium like memory, and generally closer to the consumer. There might even be varying layers of cache; for example, data can be cached in the memory of the client application and in a shared distributed cache on the backend.

When working with a cache, one of the biggest challenges is keeping the cached data synchronized with the source. When the source data changes, it is often necessary to either invalidate or update the cached copy of the data. Sometimes, the data rarely changes; in fact, in some cases the data will not change through the lifetime of the application process, making it possible to load this static data into a cache when the application starts and then not need to worry about invalidation. Here are some common approaches for cache invalidation and updates:

- Rely on TTL configurations by setting a value that removes a cached item after a configurable expiration time. The application or a service layer then would be responsible for reloading the data when it does not find an item in the cache.

- Use CDC to update or invalidate a cache. A process subscribes to a datastore change stream and is responsible for updating the cache.

- Application logic is responsible for invalidating or updating the cache when it makes changes to the source data.

- Use a passthrough caching layer that's responsible for managing cached data. This can remove the concern of the data caching implementation from the application.

- Run a background service at a configuration interval to update a cache.

- Use the data replication features of the database or another service to replicate the data to a cache.
- Caching layer renews cached items based on access and available cache resources.

Content Delivery Networks

A content delivery network (CDN) is a group of geographically distributed datacenters, also known as points of presence (POP). A CDN often is used to cache static content closer to consumers. This reduces the latency between the consumer and the content or data needed. Following are some common CDN use cases:

- Improve website loading times by placing content closer to the consumer.
- Improve application performance of an API by terminating traffic closer to the consumer.
- Speed up software downloads and updates.
- Increase content availability and redundancy.
- Accelerate file upload through CDN services like Amazon CloudFront.

The content is cached, so a copy of it is stored at the edge locations and will be used instead of the source content. In Figure 4-19, a client is fetching a file from a nearby CDN with a much lower latency of 15 ms as opposed to the 82 ms latency between the client and the source location of the file, also known as the *origin*. Caching and CDN technologies enable faster retrieval of the content, and scale by removing load from the origin as well.

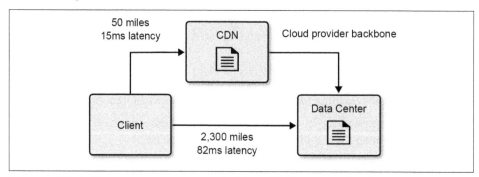

Figure 4-19. A client accesses content cached in a CDN closer to the client

The content cached in a CDN is usually configured with an expiration date-time, also known as *TTL properties*. When the expiration date-time is exceeded, the CDN reloads the content from the origin, or source. Many CDN services allow you to explicitly invalidate content based on a path; for example, */img/**. Another common

---

technique is to change the name of the content by adding a small hash to it and updating the reference for consumers. This technique is commonly used for web application bundles like the JavaScript and CSS files used in a web application.

Here are some considerations regarding CDN cache management:

- Use content expiration to refresh content at specific intervals.
- Change the name of the resource by appending a hash or version to the content.
- Explicitly expire the cache either through management console or API.

CDN vendors continue adding more features, making it possible to push more and more content, data, and services closer to the consumers, improving performance, scale, security, and availability. Figure 4-20 demonstrates a client calling a backend API with the request being routed through the CDN and over the cloud provider's backbone connection between datacenters. This is a much faster route to the API with lower latency, improving the Secure Sockets Layer (SSL) handshake between the client and the CDN as well as the API request.

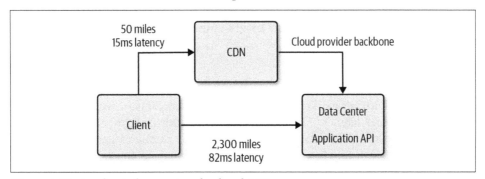

Figure 4-20. Accelerated access to a backend API

Here are a few additional features to consider when using CDN technologies:

Rules or behaviors
It can be necessary to configure routing, adding response headers, or enable redirects based on request properties like SSL.

Application logic
Some CDN vendors like Amazon CloudFront allow you to run application logic at the edge, making it possible to personalize content for a consumer.

Custom name
It's often necessary to use a custom name with SSL, especially when serving a website through a CDN.

File upload acceleration

Some CDN technologies are able to accelerate file upload by reducing the latency to the consumer.

API acceleration

As with file upload, it's possible to accelerate APIs through a CDN by reducing the latency to the consumer.

 Use a CDN as much as possible, pushing as much as you can over the CDN.

Analyzing Data

The data created and stored continues to grow at exponential rates. The tools and technologies used to extract information from data continues to evolve to support the growing demand to derive insights from the data, making business insights through complex analytics available to even the smallest businesses.

Streams

Businesses need to reduce their time to insights in order to gain an edge in today's competitive fast-moving markets. Analyzing the data streams in real time is a great way to reduce this latency. Streaming data-processing engines are designed for unbounded datasets. Unlike data in a traditional data storage system in which you have a holistic view of the data at a specific point in time, streams have an entity-by-entity view of the data over time. Some data, like stock market trades, click streams, or sensor data from devices, comes in as a stream of events that never end. Stream processing can be used to detect patterns, identify sequences, and look at results. Some events, like a sudden transition in a sensor, might be more valuable when they happen and diminish over time or enable a business to react more quickly and immediately to these important changes. Detecting a sudden drop in inventory, for example, allows a company to order more stock and avoid some missed sales opportunities.

Batch

Unlike stream processing, which is done in real time as the data arrives, batch processing is generally performed on very large bounded sets of data as part of exploring a data science hypothesis, or at specific intervals to derive business insights. Batch processing is able to process all or most of the data and can take minutes or hours to complete, whereas stream processing is completed in a matter of seconds or less.

Batch processing works well with very large volumes of data, which might have been stored over a long period of time. This could be data from legacy systems or simply data for which you're looking for patterns over many months or years.

Data analytics systems typically use a combination of batch and stream processing. The approaches to processing streams and batches have been captured as some well-known architecture patterns. The Lambda architecture is an approach in which applications write data to an immutable stream. Multiple consumers read data from the stream independent of one another. One consumer is concerned with processing data very quickly, in near real time, whereas the other consumer is concerned with processing in batch and a lower velocity across a larger set of data or archiving the data to object storage.

Data Lakes on Object Storage

Data lakes are large, scalable, and generally centralized datastores that allow you to store structured and unstructured data. They are commonly used to run map-and-reduce jobs for analyzing vast amounts of data. The analytics jobs are highly parallelizable so the analysis of the data can easily be distributed across the store. Hadoop has become the popular tool for data lakes and big data analysis. Data is commonly stored on a cluster of computers in the Hadoop Distributed File System (HDFS), and various tools in the Hadoop ecosystem are used to analyze the data. All of the major public cloud vendors provide managed Hadoop clusters for storing and analyzing the data. The clusters can become expensive, requiring a large number of very big machines. These machines might be running even when there are no jobs to run on the cluster. It is possible to shut down these clusters and maintain state for cost savings when they are not in use and resume the clusters during periods of data loading or analysis.

It's becoming increasingly common to use fully managed services that allow you to pay for the data loaded in the service and pay-per-job execution. These services not only can reduce operational costs related to managing these services, but also can result in big savings when running the occasional analytics jobs. Cloud vendors have started providing services that align with a serverless cost model for provisioning data lakes. Azure Data Lake and Amazon S3–based AWS Lake Formation are some examples of this.

Data Lakes and Data Warehouses

Data lakes are often compared and contrasted with data warehouses because they are similar, although in large organizations it's not uncommon to see both used. Data lakes are generally used to store raw and unstructured data, whereas the data in a data warehouse has been processed and organized into a well-defined schema. It's common to write data into a data lake and then process it from the data lake into a data warehouse. Data scientists are able to explore and analyze the data to discover trends that can help define what is processed into a data warehouse for business professionals.

Distributed Query Engines

Distributed query engines are becoming increasingly popular, supporting the need to quickly analyze data stored across multiple data systems. Distributed query engines separate the query engine from the storage engine and use techniques to distribute the query across a pool of workers. A number of open source query engines have become popular in the market: Presto, Spark SQL, Drill, and Impala, to name a few. These query engines utilize a provider model to access various data storage systems and partitions.

Hadoop jobs were designed for processing large amounts of data through jobs that would run for minutes or even hours crunching through the vast amounts of data. Although a structured query language (SQL)–like interface exists in tools such as HIVE, the queries are translated to jobs submitted to a job queue and scheduled. A client would not expect that the results from a job would return in minutes or seconds. It is, however, expected that distributed query engines like Facebook's Presto would return results from a query in the matter of minutes or even seconds.

At a high level, a client submits a query to the distributed query engine. A coordinator is responsible for parsing the query and scheduling work to a pool of workers. The pool of workers then connects to the datastores needed to satisfy the query, fetches the results, and merges the results from each to the workers. The query can run against a combination of datastores: relational, document, object, file, and so on. Figure 4-21 depicts a query that fetches information from a MongoDB database and some comma-separated values (CSV) files stored in an object store like Amazon S3, Azure Blob Storage, or Google Object Storage.

The cloud makes it possible to quickly and easily scale workers, allowing the distributed query engine to handle query demands.

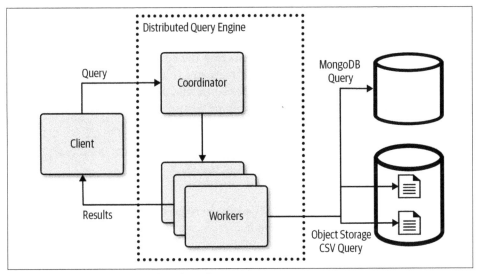

Figure 4-21. Overview of a distributed query engine

Databases on Kubernetes

Kubernetes dynamic environment can make it challenging to run data storage systems in a Kubernetes cluster. Kubernetes pods are created and destroyed, and cluster nodes can be added or removed, forcing pods to move to new nodes. Running a stateful workload like a database is much different than stateless services. Kubernetes has features like stateful sets and support for persistent volumes to help with deploying and operating databases in a Kubernetes cluster. Most of the durable data storage systems require a disk volume as the underlying persistent storage mechanism, so understanding how to attach storage to pods and how volumes work is important when deploying databases on Kubernetes.

In addition to providing the underlying storage volumes, data storage systems have different routing and connectivity needs as well as hardware, scheduling, and operational requirements. Some of the newer cloud native databases have been built for these more dynamic environments and can take advantage of the environments to scale out and tolerate transient errors.

There are a growing number of operators available to help simplify the deployment and management of data systems on Kubernetes. Operator Hub is a directory listing of operators (*https://www.opera torhub.io*).

Storage Volumes

A database system like MongoDB runs in a container on Kubernetes and often needs a durable volume with a life cycle different from the container. Managing storage is much different than managing compute. Kubernetes volumes are mounted into pods using persistent volumes, persistent volume claims, and underlying storage providers. Following are some fundamental storage volume terms and concepts:

Persistent volume

> A persistent volume is the Kubernetes resource that represents the actual physical storage service, like a cloud provider storage disk.

Persistent volume claim

> A persistent volume storage claim is a storage request, and Kubernetes will assign and associate a persistent volume to it.

Storage class

> A storage class defines storage properties for the dynamic provisioning of a persistent volume.

A cluster administrator will provision persistent volumes that capture the underlying implementation of the storage. This could be a persistent volume to a network-attached file share or cloud provider durable disks. When using cloud provider disks, it's more likely one or more storage classes will be defined and dynamic provisioning will be used. The storage class will be created with a name that can be used to reference the resource, and the storage class will define a provisioner as well as the parameters to pass to the provisioner. Cloud providers offer multiple disk options with different price and performance characteristics. Different storage classes are often created with the different options that should be available in the cluster.

A pod is going to be created that requires a persistent storage volume so that data is still there when the pod is removed and comes back up on another node. Before creating the pod, a persistent volume claim is created, specifying the storage requirements for the workload. When a persistent volume claim is created, and references a specific storage class, the provisioner and parameters defined in that storage class will be used to create a persistent volume that satisfies the persistent volume claims request. The pod that references the persistent volume claim is created and the volume is mounted at the path specified by the pod. Figure 4-22 shows a pod with a reference to a persistent volume claim that references a persistent volume. The persistent volume resource and plug-in contains the configuration and implementation necessary to attach the underlying storage implementation.

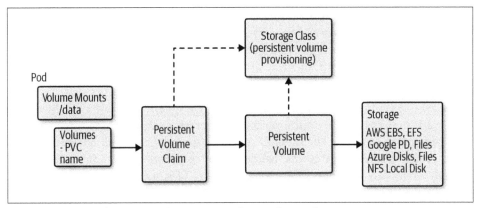

Figure 4-22. A Kubernetes pod persistent volume relationship

 Some data systems might be deployed in a cluster using ephemeral storage. Do not configure these systems to store data in the container; instead, use a persistent volume mapped to a node's ephemeral disks.

StatefulSets

StatefulSets were designed to address the problem of running stateful services like data storage systems on Kubernetes. StatefulSets manage the deployment and scaling of a set of pods based on a container specification. StatefulSets provide a guarantee about the order and uniqueness of the pods. The pods created from the specification each have a persistent identifier that is maintained across any rescheduling. The unique pod identity comprises the StatefulSet name and an ordinal starting with zero. So, a StatefulSet named "mongo" and a replica setting of "3" would create three pods named "mongo-0," "mongo-1," and "mongo-2," each of which could be addressed using this stable pod name. This is important because clients often need to be able to address a specific replica in a storage system and the replicas often need to communicate between one another. StatefulSets also create a persistent volume and persistent volume claim for each individual pod, and they are configured such that the disk created for the "mongo-0" pod is bound to the "mongo-0" pod when it's rescheduled.

 StatefulSets currently require a headless service, which is responsible for the network identity of the pods and must be created in addition to the StatefulSet.

Affinity and anti-affinity is a feature of Kubernetes that allows you to constrain which nodes pods will run on. Pod anti-affinity can be used to improve the availability of a data storage system running on Kubernetes by ensuring replicas are not running on the same node. If a primary and secondary were running on the same node and that node happened to go down, the database would be unavailable until the pods were rescheduled and started on another node.

Cloud providers offer many different types of compute instance types that are better suited for different types of workloads. Data storage systems will often run better on compute instances that are optimized for disk access, although some might require higher memory instances. The stateless services running the cluster, however, do not require these specialized instances that will often cost more and are fine running on general commodity instances. You can add a pool of storage-optimized nodes to a Kubernetes cluster to run the storage workloads that can benefit from these resources. You can use Kubernetes node selection along with taints and tolerations to ensure the data storage systems are scheduled on the pool of storage optimized nodes and that other services are not.

Given most data storage systems are not Kubernetes aware, it's often necessary to create an adapter service that runs with the data storage system pod. These services are often responsible for injecting configuration or cluster environment settings into the data storage system. For example, if we deployed a MongoDB cluster and need to scale the cluster with another node, the MongoDB sidecar service would be responsible for adding the new MongoDB pod to the MongoDB cluster.

DaemonSets

A DaemonSet ensures that a group of nodes runs a single copy of a pod. This can be a useful approach to running data storage systems when the system needs to be part of the cluster and use nodes dedicated to storage system. A pool of nodes would be created in the cluster for the purpose of running the data storage system. A node selector would be used to ensure the data storage system was only scheduled to these dedicated nodes. Taints and tolerations would be used to ensure other processes were not scheduled on these nodes. Here are some trade-offs and considerations when deciding between daemon and stateful sets:

- Kubernetes StatefulSets work like any other Kubernetes pods, allowing them to be scheduled in the cluster as needed with available cluster resources.
- StatefulSets generally rely on remote network attached storage devices.
- DaemonSets offer a more natural abstraction for running on a database on a pool of dedicated nodes.
- Discovery and communications will add some challenges that need to be addressed.

Summary

Migrating and building applications in the cloud requires a different approach to the architecture and design of applications' data-related requirements. Cloud providers offer a rich set of managed data storage and analytics services, reducing the operating costs for data systems. This makes it much easier to consider running multiple and different types of data systems, using storage technologies that might be better suited for the task. This cost and scale of the datastores has changed, making it easier to store large amounts of data at a price point that keeps going down as cloud providers continue to innovate and compete in these areas.

CHAPTER 5

DevOps

Developing, testing, and deploying cloud native applications differs significantly from traditional development and operations practices. In this chapter, you learn the fundamentals of DevOps along with the proven practices, including all of the benefits and challenges of developing, testing, and operating cloud native applications. Additionally, we cover designing cloud native applications with operations and rapid, reliable development processes in mind. Most concepts and patterns explained in this chapter are applicable to both containerized services and functions. When this is not the case, we explicitly call out the differences.

What Is DevOps?

DevOps is a broad concept that encompasses multiple aspects of collaboration and communication between software developers and other IT professionals. The easiest way to define DevOps is to talk about its goals. DevOps is intended to improve collaboration between development and operations teams throughout the entire process of software development, from planning to delivery, to improve deployment frequency, achieve faster time to market, lower the failure rate of new releases, shorten lead time between fixes, and improve mean time to recovery.

One of the models you can use when talking about DevOps is called CALMS, which stands for Collaboration, Automation, Lean, Measurement, and Sharing. The CALMS model is a method that we can use to assess, analyze, and compare the maturity of the DevOps team.

Collaboration

The collaboration in the CALMS model tells us to focus on people over processes. As an organization, you value healthy people instead of processes that can make people burn out and eventually make them quit their jobs. As part of the culture, you also embrace failure—you give people the freedom to fail and, even more important, you learn from those failures. In this culture, ideas from everyone are appreciated; you don't prefer those of only certain individuals. Hierarchy and titles do not matter, and everyone participates in the design of the system.

Automation

Automating the software cycle is crucial to be able to achieve higher deployment velocity and deployment consistency. To be able to go from an implemented feature or code change to a deployed feature in production in a matter of minutes takes a lot of reliable automation. Key elements that need to be automated are the infrastructure, Continuous Integration (CI) process, testing after you've built the code, Continuous Delivery (CD), and testing along deployment paths. Ideally, and if possible, the platform and tools you're using have the automation already built in.

Historically, setting up infrastructure was a manual process. It required people to set up the servers, configure them, deploy the applications on them, and so on. There are many drawbacks to doing things manually: the process of obtaining the hardware, setting it up, and managing it costs money; it's slow; and it has a huge impact on the ability to handle traffic spikes, for example, and launch new services or applications quickly.

One of the key benefits of the cloud is that infrastructure can be automated. Infrastructure as Code (IaC) is a method of provisioning and managing infrastructure using code rather than through manual processes. All infrastructure, such as servers, networks, and databases, is treated as code. Using code, you can create a process for configuring and deploying infrastructure components in a repeatable, consistent manner. For example, you can create scripts that you can use to deploy the servers and preconfigure different components, networks, load balancers, and any other cloud services. Simply by running this script, you consistently provision your entire infrastructure stack in a completely different region, for example. Something that would usually take weeks can be done in a matter of hours.

Lean Principles and Processes

The focus of Lean principles and processes comes from manufacturing (specifically from Toyota Production Systems). The gist with Lean is to remove any waste from your processes. An example of how to achieve this is to begin by drawing and documenting the current state of your processes. Think about what happens when you check in your code, or, what happens when you're building your servers or environments, perhaps creating a new region. How do you get from having nothing in production to having a production server/environment with your applications running? After you map all of this out, you can estimate how long each portion takes and easily spot bottlenecks, unnecessary processes, or manual processes. With these identified, you can either remove them or automate them to make the process faster. After you've repeated this a couple of times, you can come up with your desired, Lean state of processes.

Measurement

Determining whether deployments and releases are successful requires us to have specific metrics in place. The purpose of having measurements is to quickly discover any potential issues with your code or the process so that you can go back and fix it if needed. As an example, Prometheus gives you a common instrumentation point and allows developers to easily instrument code. You don't need to worry about how data is collected because there's one endpoint that polls for all data from your service. Your only worry is instrumenting and emitting metrics from within your services and functions. As you can imagine, the volume of metrics in a distributed system can be extremely high, so you also need distributed tracing tools like Jaeger or OpenTracing that allow you to correlate metrics and events throughout your services. Using these tools, you can break down calls between services and get a better view of your system, which allows you to quickly spot any bottlenecks, sources of failures, or potential optimization points.

We mentioned only the system and application measurements, but you can't forget about people metrics and the cultural aspects. Measurements inform us whether people are healthy or how investments are influencing and affecting things in the business, the amount of money it's making, or how you can innovate faster.

Additional third-party tools that can help in the area of measurements are New Relic, Splunk, and Sumo Logic. Certain cloud platforms also provide built-in metrics and tracing capabilities, such as Amazon CloudWatch and AWS X-Ray, as well as Microsoft Azure Monitor for activity logs, diagnostic logs, and metrics.

Sharing

Sharing learnings and best practices is also important, both within your organization, and between organizations in a company, as well as among your competitors and the rest of the industry with the purpose of improving the industry for everyone.

With all CALMS principles in mind, one thing they have in common is people. You can't be successful with DevOps if you're not focusing on people and ensuring that they work well together.

Testing

It probably goes without saying that any piece of code that is deployed and released into production needs to be thoroughly tested. With the velocity of deployments and releases that are commonplace for cloud native solutions, you can't survive any longer by doing manual testing. You need to automate any tests that you're planning to run because only reliable and automated tests allow you to achieve that release velocity and have confidence in your deployments and releases.

As mentioned in the previous section, CD is a DevOps practice whereby you can automatically ensure that a piece of code is production ready any time. Testing is part of the CD pipeline in which you automatically test the code, deploy it into the environment, and then release it.

To be able to do proper testing of cloud native solutions, you need to have good test automation in place. Without test automation, you can't do DevOps—automation is critical. Just as there are things you need to keep in mind when developing microservices, there are considerations around writing tests for those microservices.

How about functions? The principles for testing functions and the processes involved are similar. However, your test setup is different when testing functions.

For testing functions that are HTTP triggered and return a value, the solution is relatively simple: you trigger the function via HTTP by creating a request, invoking it, and then validating the function's response. However, you could have functions that are triggered by other events (e.g., storage queue, database operations), which don't have return values or can interact with an external system or another function. Depending on how complex the functions and your system are, you could use dependency injections or environment variables to define the endpoints, but most often you would utilize one or more *test doubles*.

Test Doubles

In most of your testing, you use either one or all of the test doubles. A test double is an object that you can use instead of a real object. For example, you could use a test double for the payment or authorization service so that you don't need to rack up charges on your credit card while testing. The three most common types of test doubles are *mocks*, *fakes*, and *stubs*.

With mocks, you can define certain expectations about how functions are called. Mocks are used for testing interactions between objects; for example, if your code uses a database, you could use a mock database instead of a real database. To test that your function writes or reads to and from the database, you set up the mock, call the function you are testing, and then verify on the mock that write or read calls were made to the database.

A fake is a lightweight implementation of your API that behaves like the real thing, but it isn't. You can use fakes when you can't use a real implementation or if using a real implementation is slow or cumbersome to set up and maintain. An example of a fake would be a fake payment or authorization service that you use in your tests.

Finally, a stub contains zero logic, and it returns only what you tell it to return. Stubs are useful if you need certain objects to return specific values and be in a particular state.

Test Automation Pyramid

Regardless of the testing context in what context, be it in cloud native architectures or monolithic architectures, you can't avoid mentioning the test automation pyramid that Mike Cohn wrote about in his blog post back in 2009.

The test automation pyramid, as shown in Figure 5-1, groups tests based on their granularity. In addition, it gives us rough guidance on the number of tests in each group.

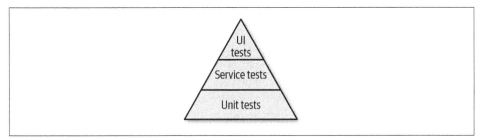

Figure 5-1. The test automation pyramid

Unit tests

The most substantial part of the pyramid, the bottom, is represented by the *unit tests*. Unit tests should be the basis of your testing and, compared to the other types of tests, you should have the most of them. If you take an example of an ecommerce website that has a login service, shipping-cost service, payment service, shopping-cart service, product catalog service, and so on, each of these services is built from multiple different modules or units that need to be covered by unit tests. With unit tests, more often than not you need to mock and fake any dependencies to be able to create different conditions under which the tested functionality runs. If you're writing unit tests for your login service, you don't want to use the actual authorization service. You also want to test the scenarios in which the authorization service is unavailable. Or, you want to test scenarios in which login didn't work, or the user doesn't exist, and so forth.

All of these scenarios become much easier to test if you use a mock service in place of the real authorization service. For each test, you can define how the mock should behave and then test your login service using that mock. When you run into issues either with writing mocks or unit tests, go back to the code and think about refactoring it to make it testable. The testable code makes your life easier in the long run. It helps you to write better unit tests and mocks that cover multiple conditions. Having a set of useful unit tests gives you confidence when making changes to that part of the code as well as when you're deploying and releasing your code to production.

Service tests

Service-level tests—which you could also call *component-level tests*—occupy the middle of the pyramid. With service-level tests, you are trying to test the service or a component as a whole, separately from the user interface (UI). For example, you would have tests that cover shipping-service functionality; the shipping service takes some inputs (an address, for example) and returns an output (shipping costs, duration, etc.).

UI tests

Finally, at the top of the pyramid are the *UI tests*. UI tests should represent the fewest number of tests of all the pyramid tests. These tests are usually costly to write and maintain; however, they are useful when testing for usability and accessibility. Let's take the ecommerce website as an example again. UI tests for the ecommerce website would include starting a browser, navigating to the website, clicking the login link, logging in, browsing through the catalog by clicking links and typing in text, and perhaps making a purchase. As you begin thinking about these tests more, you can see how complex they can become—which browsers do you use for testing? How can you reliably wait for the pages to complete loading or know when a specific action has completed? How do you make your automated UI tests resilient enough, so that they don't break if the website design or layout changes?

In addition to the aforementioned three groups of tests in the test automation pyramid, other types of tests can either fall under the service-level test group or have their dedicated slice of your test pyramid. These are the tests that you either run as part of the CD stage and each time you deploy to production, or run continuously; for example, you could have a canary test that runs continuously and exercises your application functionality in production. That way you know when something goes wrong immediately. Other types of tests (load or performance tests) can be run only on specific schedules or on demand, but not necessarily with every release.

Jepsen tests

A tool that we need to mention whenever we talk about cloud native and distributed systems is the Jepsen (*https://github.com/jepsen-io/jepsen*) library. The Jepsen library sets up a distributed system and runs a set of operations against it to verify that the history of operations makes sense. You can use Jepsen to analyze databases, coordination services, and queues, and it's able to find a plethora of issues, including data loss, stale reads, lock conflicts, and more.

Performance tests

These tests are meant to give you an idea of how your application or services are performing by measuring, for example, how long specific scenarios took. You can write performance tests on the function or unit level to measure how long a single function or request takes. In addition to lower-level performance tests, you should also consider writing a scenario or feature-level performance test that measures how long specific actions take; for example, you could measure how long the login process takes, from the time a user clicks the login button to the time they are presented with their profile or dashboard page. Almost every time you do a feature-level performance test, you need to dig deeper and have metrics and numbers on specific functions as well. This will help you to pinpoint bottlenecks and allow you to investigate why a function is taking a certain amount of time to execute. An excellent way to track performance is to establish a baseline to which you can compare all your numbers. For your baseline, you can either use the measurements obtained with the first release of your code to production or define goals that you can try to meet (e.g., "User login should not take more than X seconds for mobile users using LTE connections"). Depending on how critical performance is to your system, you can use dedicated environments and conditions within which your tests are executed and you measure your system.

Load tests

Load tests are a type of performance test that that you use to determine your system's performance under certain conditions. These conditions could be, for example, a typical load you are expecting your system to be under most of the time, or extreme or peak loads that aren't typical or expected. With load testing, you can determine the maximum load on your system and where the breaking point is. The results from the load testing can help you to plan as well as define alerting in your monitoring systems.

Security/penetration tests

The purpose of security and penetration tests is to determine whether your system is potentially vulnerable to different types of attacks and, if so, in what ways it is vulnerable. This type of testing also involves doing security reviews of system architecture to determine the possible entry points and security-critical sections. The review should also ensure services don't have unnecessary permissions and access to resources, as that can increase the fallout in case of a security breach. For example, if your service reads only from the database but never writes to it, it should have read-only access to the database and nothing more.

A/B tests

A/B tests usually are executed against services that are already running in the production environment. The purpose of an A/B test is to determine whether one version of the service (A) performs better in comparison to another service (B). If you plan to do any A/B tests, make sure that you have a well-defined goal as well as all metrics in place that allow you to measure the results. For example, you could create an A/B test to determine whether using green buttons in your call to action increases your sales (i.e., users clicking it) versus having a yellow button. As an example, you can deploy both versions of your service and equally split traffic between them. Note that equally splitting traffic is not required, and you could also pick something else as a basis for a decision to redirect someone to version A versus version B.

Acceptance tests

You can use acceptance tests to determine whether your services are ready to be moved to a different environment, for example. You could define a different set of acceptance tests before you promote the code between environments. These tests should become stricter as you move closer to the production environment.

Usability tests

Usability tests are conducted with real users of your product to discover how easy it is to use your product. Traditionally, you would come up with specific scenarios or tasks and ask your users to try to accomplish these tasks using your product. While the users are working through the tasks, you would observe them as well as have them take a survey or ask them questions after they've gone through the tasks.

Configuration tests

As the name suggests, these tests are used to validate that the configuration that is going to be applied to your services and code is correct and all in place for the service to run. For example, you want to ensure that all connection strings are defined and correct for the environment in which the service runs. You don't want to use production database connection strings for services that run in your testing or staging environment. Also, if you're doing testing in production, you need to ensure that services and functions are configured correctly so that none of the live traffic is sent to your services.

Smoke tests

Smoke tests represent a set of tests that you use to quickly determine whether a service, component, or application seems reliable enough to begin doing more thorough testing. For example, testing whether the service can successfully start and cleanly shut down is a form of a smoke test. If a service doesn't even start, there's not much other testing you can do.

Integration tests

Integration tests usually involve testing multiple different services and the interactions between them. In the test pyramid, these would be placed above service tests but under UI tests. You execute these tests in their dedicated integration environments (for example, you can have a testing environment in which all different services come together and are tested).

Chaos tests

As the name suggests, the purpose of chaos tests is to wreak havoc and introduce chaos to your system randomly. You would run a set of so-called *chaos monkeys* as a separate service within your environment to test how your system behaves when things become chaotic and services are randomly disabled, become unavailable, the network slows down, and so on. There is an entire engineering practice called *chaos engineering* that deals with identifying failures before they become outages. The idea behind chaos testing is to proactively test how your system responds to failure conditions so that you can identify and fix any issues before they become actual outages and have an impact on your customers.

Fuzz tests

Fuzz testing involves feeding a random, invalid, or unexpected set of data to your service or component in an attempt to make it fail. For example, if your service takes a JSON input, you could use existing tools to generate fuzzed JSON data or use prefuzzed data, send it to your service, and observe how it behaves.

This list of different test types is nowhere near complete; there are many other types of testing that organizations and teams do. With the sheer number of different test types, it can be tricky to know which ones to run. You could run all of them, but that wouldn't make much sense, and it would be extremely time and resource consuming. So, how do you decide which tests to run and when? With the assumption that you eventually automate all of your tests, a general guideline is to always run all unit tests on any component change and with every build. Developers should also execute unit tests as part of the pre-check-in process. After you run the unit tests, the next step would be to run acceptance, smoke, and integration tests that are affected by the changed component. These tests should be able to give you enough confidence to move the code and artifacts along to the next stage.

When to Run Which Types of Tests

Depending on the CI/CD stage your code is in, you should run different types of tests. The first tests that are usually executed are unit and service/serverless app tests. Unit tests specifically need to be small and execute in a short amount of time. Because they are run before the code merges, they serve as a first level of defense. In case of *serverless functions*, these are the tests you would run to validate each function separately.

At the next stage, the tests that can be executed either before or after code merge, depending on the complexity and how long it takes to run them, are the service-level tests. The purpose of these tests is to verify the service or the serverless application as a whole. In these tests, you will probably be using mocks instead of real service or serverless app dependencies.

After your code is merged, it is time to run integration tests. These tests verify the integration points between your services and serverless apps. To run these tests, you would deploy the services and serverless applications to their dedicated test environments and run tests between the integration points. Depending on the complexity and number of dependencies, you might want to use mocks for these tests as well. If you don't have a lot of dependencies, you could provision them in your test environment and use them only for integration tests.

Canary testing is another effective way to continuously evaluate your services and functions. You can run canary tests continuously in each environment. They should mimic the user scenarios as closely as possible and can serve as a warning system for potential issues.

The other types of tests are usually run on their own schedules or as one-offs, and they depend on the type of the services and functions you are developing. For example, it doesn't make sense to run in-person usability tests every week. These tests would be run as a one-off, probably to validate the ideas and features before releasing them or for getting feedback on features you are planning to work on.

Testing Cadence

You should execute security, fuzz, load, and performance tests at a regular interval, but it probably does not make sense to run them with each build or code change, unless the changes affect the security or performance of your system.

Before each deployment you should be running configuration tests (if any) to ensure that the service configuration is correct—you could also selectively run these tests based on whether the configuration has changed.

Chaos testing is something you do in the production environment, and you should do this at regular intervals as well. Some teams decide to do surprise chaos testing as a drill to ensure that they can handle outage situations well. The first time you run a chaos test, it's highly likely that everything will go wrong, but any subsequent runs should become easier, and there should be fewer and fewer issues discovered during this type of testing.

The usability and A/B tests fall into a category of tests that you execute when the need arises. The usability tests can be valuable each time there's a significant change to the way your product works—you want to get feedback to ensure the product is usable by your actual users. Finally, you should run A/B tests only when or if there is a need for them.

Table 5-1. Run frequency for various test types

Test type	Cadence	Notes
Unit tests	Before every code merge/check-in	Automated and fast and easy to run.
Service tests	Before (or after) every code merge/check-in	Automated and fast and easy to run, uses mocks.
Integration tests	Before deployment to staging/test environment	Automated, takes longer to run, can use mocks or real dependencies.
Canary tests	Continuously in all environments	Automated, can be costly to maintain, runs continuously.
UI tests	On UI changes	Manual; consider automating if your solution is UI heavy.
Performance tests	One-off at first, weekly later	Initial performance test might be manual and stopwatch to get a baseline. Consider automating if you can create repeatable numbers; run weekly or on bigger changes. Alert if different from baseline.
Security tests	Daily	Automated; if possible, have these tests as part of integration/canary tests. Penetration testing is usually manual and one-off. Enable vulnerability/exploit testing on the container registry.
A/B tests	As needed	Make sure you are changing one variable between A and B versions of the application to see which one is performing better.
Chaos tests	As needed	Use an automated chaos monkey tool; rerun as needed.

Testing in Production

Whenever someone mentions testing in production, it always feels like they are trying to make a joke instead of talking about it for real. However, thinking about how much investment is needed to keep multiple environments up and running—we are assuming here that you have at least a staging or testing environment—the investment for doing actual testing in production will not seem so big anymore. In our experience, the biggest problem when using separate environments for testing is merely keeping them up to date and synchronized with the actual production environment. Remember that for testing in separate environments to make sense, you need to mimic your production environment as closely as possible. This includes running pretty much everything you run in production—any databases, queues, external dependencies, and so on—and keeping all of these synchronized. For example, if you update your database version or you change the database schema, you are doing these changes twice, or rather in two environments. Besides, your testing environment is probably smaller than your production; you won't run it in each region and you won't be using the same size of compute or databases because you don't want to keep all that running, maintain it, and pay for it either.

To put it differently, your testing environment is a smaller version of your production environment—a mini-me of your production environment. This, however, can affect the way you run your services, so your per-service configuration will differ from the production service. At this point, are you testing your services in the same environment as your production services? Probably not.

Because your environment is a scaled-down version of the production, how could you even know whether that new feature or bug fix actually works the way you intended it to work? You need some monitoring in place as well, but you are effectively monitoring a completely different system, and that doesn't make much sense.

Another benefit of testing in production is that in addition to the synthetic traffic that is generated by your tests, you are also using actual customer use cases and production traffic.

It's quite clear that keeping everything running within one environment is a full-time job, let alone doing the same in two or more environments. At this point, the question about testing in production no longer sounds like a joke, and it is actually a viable solution. To be clear, we're not suggesting that testing in production is easy, not at all. There are risks, and getting to a point in your organization at which you can do this effectively involves much technical investment and possibly cultural changes as well. You should always evaluate whether making this investment is justifiable for your team or organization.

We're not saying testing environments are not valuable; they *are* valuable, and it is better than not having any testing at all. However, if you're noticing you're spending far too much time maintaining this special environment, making investments that apply only to a testing environment, or getting false positives in your tests, it makes sense for you to consider testing in production.

There are a couple of things that need to be in place before you should even consider doing testing in production. Looking at the DevOps maturity model, you should be in a place where the process of moving your code from the check-in to an environment is fully automated. That means that you are effectively doing CI and CD.

Let's break down the entire testing process into multiple stages, as shown in Figure 5-2.

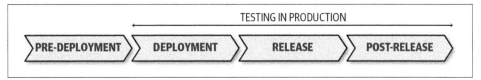

Figure 5-2. Stages of testing in production process

Let's look at each stage in more detail.

Predeployment

The services are considered in the predeployment stage after the code is built, packaged, and tagged and lives in a container image repository (such as Docker registry).

This applies similarly to your serverless applications. At this stage your functions that make up the serverless application are compiled and tests are executed. The output of this stage is an artifact, such as a ZIP package that contains the built serverless application.

Before the packaged code moves to the deployment stage, you need to run the tests mentioned earlier—unit tests, integration tests, acceptance tests, and so on—to ensure that the code meets the specific criterion and can move on to the next stage.

Deployment

Deployment is the process of taking the built, packaged, and tested code and moving it into the production environment. Practically, this means that you have generated any deployment files and other configurations that allow you to deploy the package to the platform. For serverless applications, this might involve using a declarative application model such as the AWS Serverless Application Model (AWS SAM). Your AWS SAM template defines your functions, it has a link to the built code package from the previous stage, and it can also contain any dependent services and permissions that need to be applied. One crucial difference between deploying serverless applications versus containerized services is that if you use, for example, AWS SAM templates that define everything your serverless app needs, you can quickly create multiple different environments, if needed, to test your function. Because you can create an exact replica of your production environment with low cost and you can tear it down right after you're done with it, it might be easier and less complex to do that than it would be to implement traffic routing on the function level.

One important thing to note here for containerized services is that even though your code is now in the production environment, none of the traffic is reaching it yet. Before you enable traffic to the service, you run various configuration, integration, and, possibly, load tests. After the tests pass your defined bar, you can begin releasing the service.

Release

Releasing the service involves gradually increasing the amount of real traffic you want to direct to your deployed service. If you are using containerized applications, you can quickly carry out this process by using a service mesh, such as Istio. Along with your service, you deploy a `VirtualService` resource and a `DestinationRule`. With a `DestinationRule` you define a new subset that represents the new version of your service, and in the `VirtualService` you assign the percentage of traffic that you want to run to the existing service version and the new service version. For serverless apps, you can utilize a combination of an API gateway and load balancers to achieve similar functionality. Alternatively, due to low cost and quick deployments, you can decide to create separate environments (staging, testing) for your serverless applications. If you decide to do that, make sure to define and understand which services should use which serverless applications.

For example, after deployment, you'd begin by redirecting 10% of the incoming traffic to the new version of your service. At the same time, you need to continually monitor the new service to ensure that there are no issues. In addition to monitoring, you can run additional tests that target this new service. When the test results give you enough confidence, you can increase the traffic to 20%, 50%, and, finally, to 100%. The process after increasing the traffic is the same: monitor and observe the new service and if all looks good, increase the percentage. If you discover any issues, you can decide to roll back the new release (i.e., switch traffic back to 0%), fix the issue, and then repeat the entire process. Alternatively, you can also decide to continue despite the discovered issues (provided the issues are a low priority and don't affect your service too much).

Post-release

After your service is fully released and 100% of the traffic is routed to it, you can continue doing additional tests, such as chaos tests, various A/B tests, and monitoring logs for exceptions. The post-release stage could also be called the stage at which you are operating your services. In addition to testing, this also involves responding to any exceptions and outages by having your team be on-call.

Development Environments and Tools

Development environments have traditionally been set up and configured on local development machines or virtual machines (VMs) running locally. Local development environments have enabled quick development workflows, allowing developers to quickly iterate, test, and debug code changes. Many of the tools available today have supported this approach for a long time.

The move to microservices architectures and serverless compute can make it difficult, if not impossible, to run the entire application on a local development machine. Pushing changes from local to a remote environment increases the development cycle, reducing developer productivity. It's generally been easier to quickly iterate and validate code changes locally, but new tooling is now making it increasingly easy to begin doing more of this in the cloud, or at least integrating with the cloud. There are other benefits to cloud-based development environments; they support collaboration as well as improved parity across test and production environments.

Often what's best for a team and project is some combination of local and cloud development environments and tooling. For example, some teams edit code locally, run some unit tests, and then push the changes into a cloud-based development environment. When developing a service, there are sometimes dependencies that need to run in the cloud.

Following are some development environment considerations:

- Does the code being developed need to run in the cluster?
- Where do you want to run your cluster? Locally or in the cloud?
- Where do you edit and commit changes from? Locally or in the cloud?
- Are there dependencies that need to run in the cloud?
- Is the team heavily distributed and would it benefit from collaborative development environments?

For example, a feature using serverless compute is implemented and debugged locally using unit and integration tests. Test doubles can be used to avoid having to bring up other service dependencies in the local environment. After the unit integration tests and linting are successful, the code is deployed into a dev/test environment and tested in an actual cloud environment. The changes can now be submitted in a pull request, reviewed, and moved through the CI pipeline. As Figure 5-3 demonstrates, much of the feature development is completed locally; it's the final set of verification tests in an actual cloud environment before a pull request and code review starts.

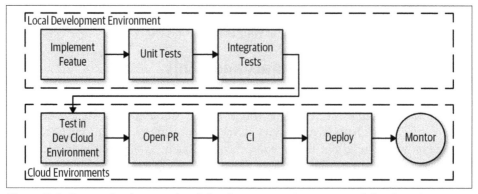

Figure 5-3. Connection between local development environment and cloud environment

Development Tools

Many useful development tools and services are now available that make it much easier to build applications with remote clusters or stand up local environments that are more similar to test and production environments. There are so many tools out there, and more showing up, that it would be difficult to cover them all.

If you are considering a local development environment, there are a couple of tools available that allow you to run Kubernetes in your local development environment:

- Minikube runs a single-node Kubernetes cluster in a VM and is commonly used for local development environments. Minikube can be useful for experimenting with Kubernetes in a local environment or setting up local development environments that are closer to test and production environments.

- Similar to Minikube, Docker for Mac and Windows is another extremely popular and easy-to-run tool that allows you to run Kubernetes locally. If you are using Docker, you probably already have this installed, and enabling Kubernetes support is as simple as selecting a checkbox in the Docker for Mac or Windows settings.

Both of these tools are useful; however, there might be features that are either not fully supported or missing in the local development scenario—for example, using the LoadBalancer type in Kubernetes services. These tools are also rapidly evolving and new features and bug fixes are added frequently, so the way Kubernetes is run locally is becoming very similar to how it is run in the production environment. Note that the local development environment is never a replacement for a real, cloud-based environment. Even though these tools will let you run the minimal Kubernetes environment on one node, you need to ensure that you have enough resources available for it to run smoothly.

In addition to the aforementioned local Kubernetes development tools, there are other useful tools available today to make local and remote development easier:

- Docker Compose is a tool for defining and running multiple containers. A YAML file is used to define the containers that you can manage, start, stop, and delete as a group. The grouping makes it easy to bring up more complex local development environments. Local container-based development environments can help isolate and avoid dependency version conflicts. The environment handles building and running the software, and the tools needed to build and run the software can be part of the image. There's no longer a need to get the right version of a runtime installed or switch between them. Dependencies on products like Redis or MongoDB can be easy to quickly bring up and down.

- KSync updates containers running on a cluster by replicating local files to the containers running in a remote cluster. A developer can use their favorite local editors and source control management tools while building, running, and testing the application in a remote cluster. Changes are replicated to a container in the cluster where they are built and run. This can sometimes make it quick to iterate on changes without the overhead of building an image, pushing it, and updating the running container.

- Skaffold is a command-line tool that you can use to continually deploy code changes to a local or remote Kubernetes cluster. It automates the development workflow by building an image and pushing it to a cluster when code changes. Skaffold can push file changes into a container if there are files that can be synchronized, or it optionally creates an image and deploys a new container instance.

- Draft is an open source tool that automates the deployment of application changes to either a remote or local Kubernetes cluster. You can use Draft to generate simple Dockerfiles and Helm charts. The tool detects the application language used when generating the files. You can customize it to streamline the development of any application or service that can run on Kubernetes. Draft makes it easy to edit locally and develop remotely.

- Telepresence is an open source tool that you can use to wire containers running locally into a remote Kubernetes cluster. This can be useful when developing multiservice applications like those used in a microservices-based architecture. You can develop a service locally, enabling fast iterations and rich debugging while transparently interacting with other services in the cluster. This works almost as if your local machine were part of the cluster.

- For Azure-specific Kubernetes development, Azure Dev Spaces is a great development tool. It allows you to develop and run containerized services in isolation directly on Azure Kubernetes Service. This isolation enables a team of developers to develop an entire application on the same development cluster collaboratively and, as a result, drastically reduces the need for mocks and stubs.

Many of the cloud vendors offering Function as a Service (FaaS) also provide local development tools, making it possible to run and debug functions locally. Amazon Web Services (AWS), for example, ships AWS Serverless Application Model (AWS SAM) Local. Microsoft's Azure Functions Core Tools includes a version of the same runtime that powers Azure Functions, which can run on a local development environment. All of these options typically use container images, so you can use Minikube or Docker for Mac/Windows to run them locally.

Development Environments

Using the tools discussed in the previous section, you can use a few different approaches to configure productive development environments that meet the needs of different teams.

Local Development Environments

Local development and debugging are still currently faster than remote, and developers are accustomed to the tools and flows of local development environments. When using one of the cloud providers' serverless compute FaaS services, you can use the cloud vendors' tools to run a local environment and/or complete the final tests in the cloud.

Docker Compose is a useful tool for setting up container-based development environments. Docker Compose can spin up the containers necessary to build and run the application as well as any dependencies such as databases. Files can be mapped to the host environment, enabling developers to use editors and source control management tools on the host system.

The following example shows a Docker Compose file that brings up a node development environment with MongoDB. The container /app directory is mapped to the current project direction and the container has access to the project source code through a volume mount. Developers will use build tools and run the application within the container but edit code files from the host system as usual:

```
version: '3'
services:
  app:
    hostname: vegeta-dev
    image: node:10.15.0
    working_dir: /app
    volumes:
      - ./:/app
    ports:
      - "3001:80"
```

```
        tty: true
        stdin_open: true
        working_dir: /app
        command: bash
        environment:
          - IP=localhost
          - PORT=8080
          - CONFIG=/app/server/config.json
        networks:
          threadsoft:
            aliases:
              - vegeta
    db:
      hostname: db
      image: mongo:4.1.6
      volumes:
        - "/data"
      networks:
        threadsoft:
          aliases:
            - db
networks:
  threadsoft:
    external:
      name: threadsoft
```

Local Development with a Remote Cluster

When using a development workflow that runs compute on a remote cluster, one of the challenges is to minimize the time it takes to push changes to the remote environment. Tools such as Skaffold, Draft, and KSync save time automating this workflow with remote Kubernetes clusters. Scripts or cloud provider frameworks might be necessary when you are developing against serverless compute FaaS. With the cloud provider FaaS, given the service deployment and code start times, it's likely faster to develop locally and run some final tests in the cloud environment.

Here are some things that you need to consider with this approach:

- Does the tool work well with an interpreted language like JavaScript or compiled languages like Go?

- Does the tool push code changes to the cloud and/or rebuild, push, and deploy?

- How long does it take to deploy and run a change? Consider experimentation before mass adoption.

Skaffold Development Workflow

You can start a Skaffold development workflow by running `skaffold dev`, which starts a deployment, and Skaffold begins watching for file changes, as seen in Figure 5-4. You can configure Skaffold to synchronize files into the running development container, like static files or the code files used in an interpreted language. If a change triggers a new build, you can configure Skaffold to build the image locally, in the cluster, or in a build service. After you execute container tests, the image is tagged, pushed to an image repository, and then deployed into the cluster. A developer can iterate on code and quickly see changes pushed to the cluster. The synchronize feature in Scaffold can save a considerable amount of time by avoiding the entire image build-push-deploy process and quickly pushing changes into the running container.

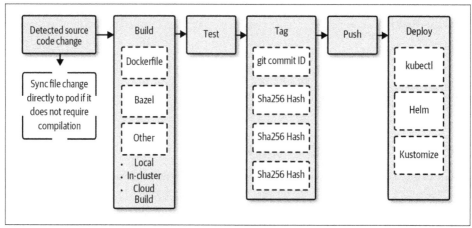

Figure 5-4. The Skaffold development workflow

By convention, Skaffold looks for a configuration file named *skaffold.yaml* in the current directory, which you can explicitly pass in by using the `--filenam` flag. A sample Skaffold file is presented in the following example, which configures Skaffold to synchronize *.js* files into the running container and deploy using `kubectl` with the *k8s-pod.yaml* Kubernetes pod specification:

```
apiVersion: skaffold/v1beta4
kind: Config
build:
  artifacts:
  - image: gcr.io/my-project/node-example
    context: .
    sync:
      '*.js': .
deploy:
  kubectl:
```

```
manifests:
- "k8s-pod.yaml"
```

 When deploying into Kubernetes, this flow also works against local development clusters, like a Minikube cluster.

Remote Cluster Routed to Local Development

In this development flow, a service is developed locally just like the local development flow. The Telepresence tool runs a proxy in the remote cluster and is an ambassador for the local service, proxying requests through to the local service and back out to other services in the cloud.

Figure 5-5 depicts a request from one service routed to the Telepresence proxy as though it were the actual service. The Telepresence proxy sends the request to the service running in the local development environment. A request is made from the service being developed in the local development environment to another in the cluster, and Telepresence handles proxying this request to the actual service in the cluster. Telepresence also replicates cluster environment settings like configurations to the service running in the local development environment. This replication can be useful when you need to develop and debug a service locally while other service dependencies run in the remote cloud environment.

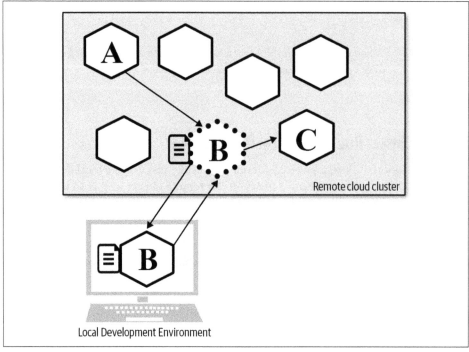

Figure 5-5. Developing locally against a remote cloud cluster

Cloud Development Environments

With the cloud development environments, developers connect to development machines running in the cloud. Integrated development environments (IDEs) are either browser based or accessed through a remote virtual desktop–type environment. Tools like Eclipse Che are able to provision developer workspaces in a cluster. This helps ensure consistency across developer workspace environments and makes it easy to bring up new developer environments.

CI/CD

CI is a practice of automated building, testing, and integrating newly developed code with the existing code for the purpose of releasing it. In practical terms, this means building the code in your feature branch, running unit tests, merging the code if it passes, and, finally, creating an artifact, such as a binary, a container image, or a compressed file, depending on your type of service. CI ensures that any code that you are trying to merge to the master or release branch has passed a series of tests—it gives you a certain degree of confidence and allows you to catch any issues early on. As part of the CI process, your code is packaged, tagged, and pushed to a container registry (like Docker Registry), and instead of moving the code between different stages, you are moving only the container image information (e.g., container image registry and container image name with corresponding tags), which significantly speeds up the entire process.

You can think of the next phase, CD, as an addition to the CI. In this phase, you are running additional tests with the goal of having your code always ready to be deployed to production. In practical terms, after your code passes through this stage, there shouldn't be any questions about its stability or quality, and any engineer could easily deploy code to production.

By the time your code reaches the final phase, called Continuous Deployment, it is thoroughly tested and it can be automatically deployed to your production environment. Compared to CD, this phase is all about automated deployment without any manual intervention. Some teams stop at the CD phase and decide to do manual deployments to production.

As an engineer, having all three phases in place gives you peace of mind that if your code is merged and it passes the tests and the delivery phase, it is automatically deployed to production. Assuming that you have this in place for your entire system and its components, it enables you to independently deploy any parts of the system multiple times with high confidence.

Regardless of whether you're working with services or serverless applications and functions, you would be using the same CI/CD process. The fact that a function is usually smaller than a service doesn't change the way they are treated when they are built or deployed.

Figure 5-6 shows a couple of different stages that are part of your CI/CD process.

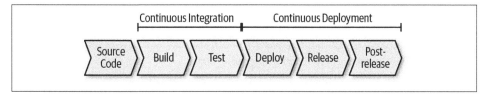

Figure 5-6. Stages of the CI/CD process

Source Code Control

Source control is where everything begins in the CI/CD flow. It is the repository in which your code resides. There are multiple ways in which your source code control could be set up, but you should have at least a main branch called "master" and probably multiple other branches where you do your feature work and bug fixes. Your source code control is the source of truth for your code and, if you desire, configuration as well.

How About Mono-Repo and Multi-Repo?

The idea behind the mono-repo is to store all of your code (all services, tools, application, etc.) in a single source code repository. The alternative to the mono-repo is a multi or poly-repo in which your code is in multiple repositories; for example, each service or function resides in its repository, tools in a separate repository, and so on. It is difficult to give a final suggestion on which option is better, because regardless of which way you go, you need to solve similar problems. On top of that, the choice depends on multiple other factors, such as the number of services you have.

One of the benefits of having all your code in one repository is that it enables better and easier collaboration and sharing of code. As a developer, you won't need to chase different repositories and try to correlate changes across multiple repositories because everything is in one place. On the other hand, why would you need to clone one, huge mono-repo if you are working on or interested in only a small piece of it or a single service? As you can see, it can be difficult to make a recommendation on which way to go. If the number of services and code is relatively small, it makes more sense to keep it in a single repository, in which case, it does make collaboration easier, and you have everything in one place. However, as soon as the size of the repository and number of services exceed a certain number, it makes more sense to split the mono-repo into multi-repos.

Another thing to consider is how your services are built and how you are going to manage service dependencies. Having everything in one repository can push you toward more code reuse and, potentially, tight coupling as well as dependency sharing. It can quickly get out of hand, so if you're considering a mono-repo, carefully consider how dependency management works and make sure you are correctly isolating services and avoiding tight coupling. Also, think about what happens if there's a build break that's not necessarily in the portion of the mono-repo you own. Is the entire build broken or just that one part? You can solve all of this with tools; however, you get this guarantee for free when using multi-repos.

With regard to building the mono-repo and producing build artifacts/container images, you can get a single version/tag that is used for all of your services, and this can make your testing easier because you are using a single name to refer to the collection of services and state of the world. Using multi-repos, you end up with different tags for each artifact, and your "state of the world" becomes a collection of different services, tags, and versions. Having a mono-repo can also help if you're deploying all services at the same time. However, this is probably not the result you want. With cloud native, you should be striving to get to a place where you can independently deploy each service. Keeping this goal in mind, having all of your services in a mono-repo doesn't give you any apparent benefits.

In terms of code ownership, a mono-repo makes it difficult to define where the boundaries are. With multi-repos, it is much clearer which teams own what and who's responsible for which part of the code.

Build Stage (CI)

Regardless of how your repositories are structured and how many of them you have, the purpose of the build stage is to take all of the changes you committed to your repository and build the code to ensure that there are no errors in it. If the build succeeds, you move to the next stage where your code is tested. If a build fails, the entire process stops, code changes are rejected, and the developer is notified.

Test Stage (CI)

In this stage of the pipeline, you know the code was successfully built, but now it's time to run the range of tests, including unit tests, functional tests, acceptance tests, static analysis, linting, acceptance tests, and so forth. This part of the CI process falls under the predeployment stage of testing in the production process.

After you execute the tests and they pass, the code is packaged and tagged with a version number or commit ID and pushed to a container image repository or, in the case of a serverless application, packaged and uploaded to storage. If tests failed, the code check-in is rejected, and the developer is notified. This stage concludes the CI process.

Because you are testing and building your code often, it makes sense to ensure that both build and test stages are fast and the generated artifact is as small as possible to make it easier to move around. In addition, the artifact should also be reusable so that you don't need to rebuild the same container image multiple times. If you're using Docker, you should take advantage of the multistage build process in which you build your code using a container image that has everything that's needed for the build to happen. In the second stage of your build, you copy only the built artifact to the release container image. Ideally, the release container image includes your built service and nothing else, which makes the resulting container image smaller.

Here's is a basic example of how a Dockerfile with multistage build would look if you were using Golang:

```
FROM golang:1.11.5
WORKDIR /go/src/github.com/peterj/simplego
COPY main.go .
RUN CGO_ENABLED=0 GOOS=linux go build -a -installsuffix cgo -o app .
FROM alpine:latest
RUN apk --no-cache add ca-certificates
WORKDIR /root/
COPY --from=0 /go/src/github.com/peterj/simplego/app . CMD ["./app"]
```

The previous Dockerfile uses the `golang:1.11.5` container image and copies the source file to the container first, then uses `go build` to build a binary called *app*. In the bottom part of the code, you define a second container image based on the Alpine container image, install the `ca-certificates`, and copy the built binary from the first stage of the build (`--from=0`). Finally, you run the binary using the `CMD` command.

If you build this, you end up with a final container image with a size around 8 MB, whereas the container image in the first stage of the build is more than 800 MB. The 100-fold size difference is significant, and you can imagine the difference in speed when this container image is moved around between registries or is pulled to different hosts. The majority of popular Docker images on the Docker Hub image registry have a full-sized image available in addition to the smaller or trimmed-down versions, usually tagged with the word *slim*.

From the security standpoint, smaller images also mean a smaller attack surface given that the only thing your image contains is your binary and nothing else. If you're using a full-sized operating system image (e.g., Ubuntu) to install your binaries on top of it, the potential attackers gain access to your binary as well as the whole assortment of tools that come with the Ubuntu operating system.

One of the best practices for tagging the container image is to use an abbreviation of the Git commit checksum hash and a build number. Following this naming practice, a sample container image name looks like this: *myimage: ed3ee93-1.0.0*. Using this naming format, you can quickly discover which changes the image contains. After you decide to make the container images public and available for others, you can remove the hash and use only the version number, like this: *myimage:1.0.0*. Whenever you push a new version of the image to a public container image registry, make sure that you also create the *latest* tag, which references the latest version of the image.

Testing serverless applications involves running a similar set of tests as for containerized applications—unit tests, integration tests, acceptance tests, and so on. For unit tests, you should mock any dependencies your functions have; however, to run integration tests, you can create a test environment in which you trigger test events that will in turn execute and exercise your functions. The important thing to have set up for your serverless applications is a template that describes the environment and any dependencies your functions have. Using this template, you can quickly create and tear down an environment. Because this is a short-lived environment meant for testing only, the cost will be significantly lower than constantly maintaining a test or staging environment. For serverless applications, the output of this stage would be a tested and packaged artifact that contains your serverless application.

Deploy Stage (CD)

The deploy stage of the process can be automatically triggered by the successful completion of the CI stage or, in the case of a containerized application, an event that is triggered when a new container image is pushed to the container image repository. An important thing to note is that after you reach the deploy stage, you are no longer dealing with source code, but container images, packaged artifacts, and configuration and deployment templates.

The purpose of the deploy stage is to take the built and tested artifact and deploy it to the desired environment (production, for example, or the staging environment). If you take Kubernetes as your deployment platform, this stage would involve creating all deployment and configuration files that are needed to deploy the artifact into Kubernetes. At this stage, you can use Helm and templatized deployment files with a custom set of configuration and values to deploy the artifact. If you're deploying to production, your configuration also includes a service mesh or other configuration needed to ensure that no traffic or requests are sent to the deployed container image. The configuration depends on what type of tests are you going to run: if you're planning to run load tests or additional integration tests, you need a set of configuration files that allow only testing traffic to pass to the deployed container image.

For serverless applications, assuming that you are using AWS Lambda, you can use AWS SAM to define your application, point to the packaged artifact, and include any additional infrastructure (API gateways) and permissions. Creating a test or staging environment for serverless applications is trivial if you're using one of the templating solutions that are available from cloud providers.

Another pattern and type of testing that's popular is called traffic mirroring, shadowing, or dark traffic. What this allows you to do is to mirror or shadow all real and production-level traffic and send it to the deployed service. Note that you are not routing the production traffic through the newly deployed service; the real traffic still goes through your released service, and in addition to that, it also is mirrored to the deployed service.

If you're using Istio as your service mesh, you can enable traffic mirroring by adding the mirror key to your Istio virtual service resource. Here's an example of a virtual service that sends all traffic to the released (v1) service but also mirrors all requests to the deployed (v2) service:

```
apiVersion: networking.istio.io/v1alpha3
kind: VirtualService
metadata:
  name: recommendation-service
spec:
  hosts:
    - recommendation-service
  http:
  - route:
    - destination:
      host: recommendation-service
      subset: v1
```

```
        weight: 100
    mirror:
        host: recommendation-service
        subset: v2
```

With the mirroring in place, you can run additional tests, or instead use the production traffic and monitor the deployed service. You can achieve similar functionality for your serverless applications with AWS CodeDeploy, for example, or Azure Traffic Manager. These solutions can help you to gradually shift traffic from one version to another and do blue/green deployments.

If you are not doing testing in production, your deployment at this stage would have been into a dedicated staging or testing environment. Because of that, you could automatically begin redirecting 100% of the traffic to the new service and release it as soon as it is deployed, effectively combining the deploy and release stages. As your final step in the process, you would be carefully monitoring the service as well as the entire environment as you're running the tests. Upon successful completion of the test, you would start a separate CD process that would take the container image from the staging or test environment and deploy and release it into the production environment.

Release Stage (CD)

To get started with this stage, you should have gathered enough data from testing the deployed service to feel comfortable with beginning to release the service to production.

As mentioned previously, the process of releasing involves slowly redirecting a portion of the production traffic to the service or swapping a staging deployment slot with a production deployment slot. Redirecting production traffic could be easily achieved using a service mesh such as Istio for containerized services or using AWS CodeDeploy or Azure Traffic Manager for doing the same with serverless applications. In both cases, you can gradually increase traffic to the new service or serverless application until you are directing 100% of the traffic to the new version. You have multiple options of picking and choosing the production traffic that you redirect. Usually, you would take a percentage of all production traffic and redirect it. However, in some cases, you could be more selective and smartly pick the traffic, based on the features in your new service. For example, if your service contains a fix for an issue that occurs only in a certain web browser, you could decide to redirect only traffic coming from the affected web browsers to your service. That way you can verify that the issue is fixed with the real users. Note that you probably want to test with other traffic as well, because you don't want to introduce issues for other browsers.

Similarly, you could get even fancier and more advanced and route traffic based on specific HTTP headers. For example, you could introduce a unique header name and value that gives users access to beta features of your product. Then, with the beta releases, you can route only the users who have opted into the newly released service. This could also be done for serverless applications at the API gateway level.

Regardless of how you decide to pick the production traffic, you need to carefully monitor and observe released services and functions each time you increase the percentage of the production traffic to the new version. If you discover any issues, you can change the production traffic split and restore the previous state for which all traffic was going to the previously released version. Alternatively, you can also decide to remove the new version from production by doing the reverse process of deployment. If you observe that the new version is behaving well and there are no new issues introduced, you can keep increasing the traffic, and when you reach 100%, you have successfully released a new version.

In the perfect, ideal world, the decision to increase the traffic to the new version is made automatically for you. There would be systems in place that could intelligently decide to move forward with the release, based on the data received from the service. A fully automated workflow like this is a part of the mature DevOps stage in which you're doing CI, CD, and Continuous Deployment. However, the reality is that this is a manual process, and user intervention is required to make a decision as to whether to move to the new version.

When you reach 100% of traffic to the new service, you can remove the previously released (now deployed) service from the environment and enter the final stage of the process, called post-release.

Post-Release Stage

In some sense, this stage doesn't fall under CD; however, it is a part of testing in production or operating any application in production. The post-release stage is a stage in which all of your released applications are in, and it involves continuous service monitoring, investigating incident and error reports received from the users directly or through your alerting and monitoring system, as well as doing additional testing such as chaos tests.

Here are some of the key items to keep in mind when building out your own CI/CD pipeline:

- Builds should be fast (mono-repo or poly-repo)
- Tests should be reliable
- Container images should be as small as possible
- Decide on the production traffic selection strategy (all traffic, portion of the traffic, based on specific criteria, etc.)
- Observable services are essential to a successful CI/CD pipeline

Monitoring

We have mentioned the importance of having proper monitoring and observable services throughout this chapter. Without monitoring you are effectively flying blind, not knowing what your service is doing or how is it behaving. Monitoring is essential during all stages of the CI/CD process; however, it's especially important during the release stage.

Monitoring is traditionally used to assess and report on the overall health of a system or services. Let's take a look at some of the primary metrics in monitoring:

Error rate
> This metric should tell you the rate of requests that are failing (e.g., number of HTTP 500).

Incoming request rate
> Usually measured in HTTP requests per second (or reads/writes/transactions per time unit if this is a database), it indicates how much traffic is coming into your system.

Latency
> Latency is the time it took for your service to process a request. The latency is usually broken down to successful and unsuccessful requests.

Utilization
> Utilization gives you information about the usage of different pieces of your system. For example, you would monitor utilization of the nodes in the Kubernetes cluster—making sure memory, disk, and CPU usage are in normal ranges.

During a release, if you observe any negative impact on the listed metrics, for example, error rate increases, it should be a clear sign that something is not right, and you would need to stop and roll back the release. Your monitoring should give you information and data that allows you to understand what or which part of your system is broken and why is it broken.

It is best to come up with a set of metrics (basic listed metrics and any additional metrics that you deem necessary for your service) before you do your first release. With this set in place, you can monitor your releases and don't need to guess or scramble if anything goes wrong. You should also probably define what changes in the metrics would warrant a rollback and, similarly, how long to monitor these metrics and how to decide when to continue with the release process. For example, you could decide that if there's more than a 1% change in a negative direction (or even a slight change in negative direction) in any of the listed metrics, you'll stop and roll back the release. Similarly, you can define that if there are no adverse changes in the listed metrics in the next 24 hours, you will continue with the release process and route even more production traffic to it.

In most of the cases, only a couple of metrics are enough to decide to continue or roll back the release. If you're doing A/B testing, for example, the basic set of health metrics is usually not enough, and you need to rely on more data from the services or the whole system.

One of the favorite tools for monitoring is Grafana (*https://grafana.com*), described as "the open platform for beautiful analytics and monitoring." It can use different data sources and visualize them with appealing graphs, tables, heat maps, and other visual elements. It also features a powerful query language that you can use to create advanced and customized graphs, as demonstrated in Figure 5-7.

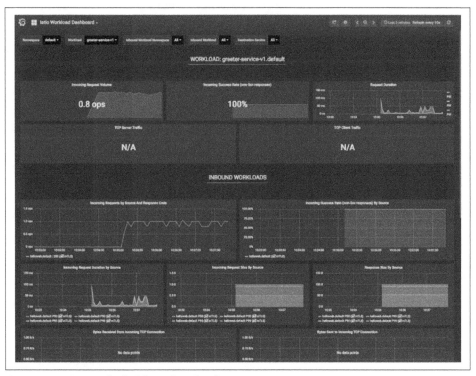

Figure 5-7. A sample dashboard in Grafana

Grafana can connect to different data sources and databases and allows you to create dashboards and graphs based on that data. One of the quite popular and built-in data source plug-ins in Grafana is for Prometheus (*https://prometheus.io*).

Collecting Metrics

A Cloud Native Computing Foundation (CNCF)–graduated project, Prometheus is a popular option used for scraping and collecting metrics from your services. Prometheus is containerized, so you can quickly run it as a container in your Kubernetes platform. Note that for Prometheus to work, you need to define a data volume where scraped metrics are stored as well as create a configuration file that defines things like scraping intervals, timeouts, and different rules and alerts. Of course, you also need to add instrumentation code to your services; otherwise, there's nothing for Prometheus to do.

There are client libraries available for most of the popular languages, and these libraries allow you to define and expose metrics via an HTTP endpoint. Prometheus then calls this HTTP endpoint, and your service sends the tracked metrics to Prometheus for storage. There's also support for a so-called push gateway—if your components cannot be scraped, you can use the push gateway to push the data to a component that Prometheus can scrape. Alternatively, you could look for an exporter—this is a component that helps with exporting metrics from third-party systems as Prometheus metrics. For example, there are exporters available for databases (MongoDB, MySQL, Redis), messaging systems (Kafka, RabbitMQ), APIs (GitHub, Docker Hub), logging components (Fluentd), as well as software, such as Kubernetes, etcd, Grafana, and more.

Let's look at an example of how easy it is to create and emit a simple metric using Golang. In this example, you define a /hello HTTP endpoint that displays a message and a metric that tracks how often the endpoint is called. Here are the contents of the *main.go* file:

```go
package main
import (
    "fmt"
    "github.com/prometheus/client_golang/prometheus"
    "github.com/prometheus/client_golang/prometheus/promauto"
    "github.com/prometheus/client_golang/prometheus/promhttp"

    "log"
    "net/http"
)

var helloCounter = promauto.NewCounter(prometheus.CounterOpts{
    Name: "hello_endpoint_total_calls",
    Help: "The total number of calls to the /hello endpoint",
})

func main() {
    http.Handle("/metrics", promhttp.Handler())
    http.HandleFunc("/hello", func(w http.ResponseWriter, r *http.Request) {
        fmt.Fprintf(w, "Hello")
        helloCounter.Inc()
    })
    log.Fatal(http.ListenAndServe(":8080", nil))
}
```

Let's walk through the source and explain what's happening. At the beginning of the file, the Prometheus Golang client library is imported. Next, you create a variable called helloCounter—this is one of the Prometheus metric types—which has a name and a help text that explains what this metric represents. Prometheus also supports other types of metrics:

Counter

> This metric type represents an increasing counter that starts at zero. You should use it only for values that increase. You can use this metric to count the number of requests, errors, restarts, and more.

Gauge

> Similar to counter, but the value in this metric can be increased or decreased. You can use this metric to represent memory, CPU usage, process count, and more.

Histogram

> You use the histogram metric type for sampling observations (request/response sizes, durations, etc.) that are then counted and placed in multiple configurable buckets. When scraped, a histogram provides cumulative counters for each bucket, information about the total sum of all observed values, and a count of events.

Summary

> The summary is similar to the histogram. In addition to what the histogram provides, the summary also calculates configurable quantiles over a sliding time window.

Let's continue by looking at the main function where two endpoints are defined: the /metrics endpoint and /hello endpoint. The /metrics endpoint is what the Prometheus scraper calls to get the state of the metrics from the application, and the /hello endpoint is where the hello_endpoint_total_calls counter is increased.

After you build and run the application, you can call the /metrics endpoint. Apart from numerous other metrics and values, the one metric you added is also in the response:

```
...
# HELP go_threads Number of OS threads created.
# TYPE go_threads gauge
go_threads 7
# HELP hello_endpoint_total_calls The total number of calls to the /hello endpoint
# TYPE hello_endpoint_total_calls counter
hello_endpoint_total_calls 0
...
```

Notice the hello_endpoint_total_calls metric shows up in the list when the /metrics endpoint is called, and the value set in the counter is 0 because there were no calls made to the /hello endpoint yet. After you make a couple of calls to the /hello endpoint and access the /metric endpoint again, the value changes, for example:

```
hello_endpoint_total_calls 5
```

Now that the service is emitting metrics, how can you configure a Prometheus scraper that automatically scrapes the data from the endpoint? As with almost everything in cloud native, there is a Prometheus Docker image available that you can use for this. Prometheus is configured using a *prometheus.yml* configuration file. Here's a minimal configuration file that defines the scrape configuration:

```
global:
scrape_interval: 5s
scrape_configs:
- job_name: 'prometheus'
static_configs:
- targets: ['hello-svc:8080']
```

The most crucial part in the previous configuration is the scrape_configs section—this is what tells Prometheus where to look for the /metrics endpoint. Under the scrape_config, a single static config is defined, and it contains the service DNS name (the assumption being that this is deployed to Kubernetes). The configuration file can be stored within the ConfigMap Kubernetes resource and then deployed:

```
apiVersion: v1
kind: ConfigMap
metadata:
  name: prom-config
  labels:
    name: prom-config
data:
  prometheus.yml: |-
    global:
      scrape_interval: 5s
      scrape_configs:
        - job_name: 'prometheus'
          static_configs:
            - targets: ['hello-svc:8080']
```

Similarly, you create a Kubernetes service and deployment for both the application and Prometheus. Here's an example of a deployment resource that pulls in the Prometheus ConfigMap created earlier:

```
apiVersion: extensions/v1beta1
kind: Deployment
metadata:
    name: prometheus
spec:
    replicas: 1
    template:
```

```
metadata:
    labels:
        app: prometheus
spec:
    containers:
        - image: prom/prometheus
          args:
            - "--config.file=/etc/prometheus/prometheus.yml"
            - "--storage.tsdb.path=/prometheus/"
          imagePullPolicy: Always
          name: prometheus
          ports:
              - containerPort: 9090
          volumeMounts:
            - name: prom-config-volume
              mountPath: /etc/prometheus
            - name: prom-storage-volume
              mountPath: /prometheus/
    volumes:
        - name: prom-config-volume
          configMap:
            defaultMode: 420
            name: prom-config
        - name: prom-storage-volume
          emptyDir: {}
```

In addition to the deployment, you could also create a Kubernetes service to access the Prometheus instance or use the `port-forward` command in the Kubernetes CLI to get access to one of the Prometheus pods. To get the pod name, run the following command, which saves the name of the Prometheus pod in the `PROMPOD` variable:

```
export PROMPOD=$(kubectl get po --selector=app=prometheus -o
custom-columns=:metadata.name --no-headers=true)
```

With the pod name in `PROMPOD`, run the following command to forward the local port 9090 to the port 9090 on the container:

```
kubectl port-forward pod/$PROMPOD 9090
```

To validate that Prometheus is scraping the defined target, open your browser and navigate to *http://localhost:9090*. You should see a page similar to the one depicted in Figure 5-8.

If all is set up correctly, the state of the *http://hello-svc:8080/metrics* endpoint should read UP.

Finally, let's check whether the metrics are being scraped. To do that, navigate to *http://localhost:9090* and then, from the drop-down menu next to the Execute button, select the metric name, `hello_endpoint_total_calls`, and click the Execute button. This runs the query and shows the value of the selected metric.

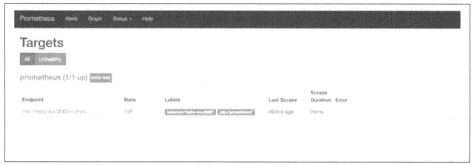

Figure 5-8. Status page for Prometheus scraping targets

Alerting

Prometheus also supports defining alerts using a separate component called Alert-manager. Any alerts defined in Prometheus are sent to the Alertmanager, and they are managed by it. Alertmanager then takes care of silencing, aggregating, and sending notifications through email or other services (e.g., Slack, PagerDuty).

In the Alertmanager configuration, you can define different routes with receivers and matches. You can get granular with alerting rules and define them based on specific services. For example, you could configure alerts in such a way that anytime an alert occurs for your frontend services, a PagerDuty account is notified and a person is paged with high urgency. Similarly, you could decide to send only a Slack message if an alert occurs for services running in your development environment.

As a basic guideline, all of your alerts should be simple: you want them to be easily understandable so that when an alert fires at 3 AM, the engineer that needs to handle it can quickly determine what the alert is about. Similarly, don't set up page alerts for everything—no one wants to be woken up in the middle of the night for an issue that easily could wait until the morning when most of the team is awake.

When defining your alert, don't forget to include a link to the web page or a document that explains and details what triggered the alert and how to resolve it.

Observable Services

Observability captures everything that monitoring doesn't—if metrics were the gist of the talk in the monitoring context, traces are what are talked about in the observability context. Monitoring is used to report the overall system's health and is, in general, more high level. On the other hand, observability gives you more granular details and insights into your services and systems along with any details and additional data (logs, exceptions, error messages) that can help you debug the service more effectively. Practically speaking, monitoring informs you that something is wrong with your service (e.g., success rate dropped, error rate increased), and observability helps you dig deeper, provide traces, and investigate why monitoring giving you those results. One of the reasons why you want to make your services observable is to be able to get data that helps you understand them better.

Logging

Logging is a crucial part that can help make your service and functions more observable. Here are some general considerations to keep in mind when developing services and functions:

- Use structured logging so that tools and automation can parse it.
- Log entries should be easy to read, and clear, concise, and provide value.
- Use the same time zone and time format for all timestamps.
- Categorize log entries: debug, info, and error are good ones to start with.
- Never log any private or sensitive information (passwords, connection strings). If you can't avoid logging it, ensure that you scrub it.

When thinking and talking about logging in the cloud native world, the first thing that should come to your mind is the sheer volume of the log messages that are generated. With cloud storage, you can store all of this data in a cost-effective way and even use automatic data archiving and long-term backups for your logs, such as Amazon Simple Storage Service (Amazon S3) Glacier. Even though storage can be cheap, having clean, parsable, and easily understandable logs should still be your priority. Getting to that place requires you to understand your services well. In any case, all logs that are generated need to be collected and stored in a central place where you can use different monitoring tools (Grafana, Kibana) or log analysis and management tools such as Loggly, Sumo Logic or Splunk to make use of that vast amount of data. If you don't do this, you quickly realize that you're not getting much value from your logs at all, especially if you need to collect them separately from each service and then try to correlate them.

After all your logs flow into a central system, you need to ensure that every log entry contains a unique identifier (request ID, correlation ID [CID]) that you can use to trace the requests and calls across services. Ideally, this unique ID is something you would also report to the users in case they run into issues. That way, you can go to your log aggregator, type in that unique ID, and be presented with all of the relevant log entries from across your entire system. Similarly, distributed tracing tools can use the identifiers to stitch together different requests that happen between services in the system.

Distributed tracing

Distributed tracing is a way to profile and monitor services, and it can help you uncover failures and poor performance as well as help you debug your services.

OpenTracing strives to create standardized APIs and instrumentation for distributed tracing. It is a collection of frameworks and libraries that implement the specification, and it allows you to add instrumentation to your code using APIs that don't lock you into a specific product or vendor. The OpenTracing specification is open sourced, and anyone can contribute or implement it within their tools.

Any distributed trace contains one or more spans that represent a single unit of work happening within a distributed system. Each span contains a name, a start and finish timestamp, tags, logs, and a context, as well as references to other spans. These values are used to stitch the spans together into a complete trace that shows how a request travels through the distributed system.

One of the popular distributed tracing tools that can visualize collection traces and spans is Jaeger (*https://www.jaegertracing.io*). In addition to stitching traces together, Jaeger also shows you all services involved in the call as well as how long each portion of the request took, as shown in Figure 5-9.

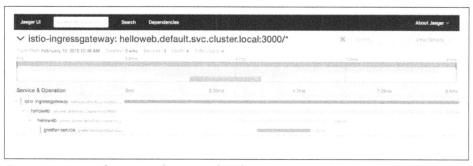

Figure 5-9. A sample trace in the Jaeger distributed tracing tool

If you're using the Istio service mesh, you can get Jaeger and install and configure it as part of Istio. With Jaeger installed, you can very quickly get started with distributed tracing. Istio Envoy proxies send all traces automatically, but you still need to provide some hints in your service calls so that Jaeger can correlate all calls correctly. If you decide to use Jaeger and distributed tracing in your services, make sure that you add and forward these headers on to any downstream service you're calling from your service:

- x-request-id
- x-b3-traceid
- x-b3-spanid

- x-b3-parentspanid
- x-b3-sampled
- x-b3-flags
- x-ot-span-context

You should also come up with a standard format for each log entry so that you can always get the necessary information from any entry. For example, in addition to the unique ID, you could also include things like timestamp and the name of the component, service, or function that created the log entry. A simple example of a single log entry with some standard information would look like this:

```
{
"id": "45b2659d-e039-49c6-9052-d6d0f79bb03a",
"timestamp": "2019-02-07T18:51:12.013594455Z",
"logLevel": "info",
"serviceId": "hello-svc",
"msg": "sample log message here"
}
```

You could also decide to create a common structure of log entries based on different types of log messages. For example, if your system is handling events, you could create an entry type called Event, and that log entry includes any event-specific information, such as eventName and eventType, as well as the standard fields mentioned earlier. Similarly, your log entries for errors should have common fields like error Code, errorName, and stacktrace.

There are unique challenges for serverless apps regarding tracing. The resources typically exist only during execution, and compared to microservices, there are no hosts in serverless where you can install agents for monitoring or tracing. Another challenge associated with collecting metrics in real time is the latency overhead as well as correlating everything across all services and functions.

For tracing of serverless apps, you can use one of the cloud providers' managed solutions such as AWS X-Ray or Azure Application Insights. These solutions collect traces from each service the request passes through. The tracers are recorded and correlated to give you a map of calls including the trace data such as latency, HTTP status, and other request metadata. With all of this information in one place, you can drill into the specific requests to analyze and identify root causes for any issues. For example, if you are using Lambda, the X-Ray agent is natively built in to it, meaning that you don't need to do anything other than enable tracing in configuration. This will allow you to identify function initialization and cold starts as well as pinpoint any issues in downstream services your function is calling. Even if you're not using Lambda, there are X-Ray SDKs available and you can use them to instrument your own services and functions.

Service health, liveness, and readiness

Your service should also include so-called *health* or *liveness* endpoints. This endpoint, when called, should respond with a value (usually HTTP 200) that indicates whether the service considers itself healthy. The endpoint name should be unique across all of your services (/health or /healthz) and when invoked should return the same structured response that quickly can be used to determine whether the service is healthy.

This health check can then be utilized by the platform to assert whether the service is healthy; if it isn't, the platform can decide to mark the service as unhealthy. Here's a snippet of how you can define the liveness probe on your service when running in Kubernetes:

```
livenessProbe:
  httpGet:
    path: /healthz
    port: 8080
  initialDelaySeconds: 5
  periodSeconds: 3
```

With the snippet, you are instructing the Kubernetes platform to wait for 5 seconds before doing the first check, and then to repeat that check every 3 seconds. If the ++$$/$$healthz++ endpoint returns a success code (HTTP 200), the service is considered alive and healthy. If the endpoint returns a non-200 code, the service is killed and restarted.

In addition to the health check endpoint, you can also include a *readiness* endpoint. The purpose of this endpoint is to determine whether the service is ready to start receiving requests from other services. When this endpoint is invoked, you could do certain checks to ensure that all service dependencies are up and accessible and ascertain whether the service can start receiving requests. Similar to the health check, some platforms support a readiness check and only start routing requests to your service after it's ready. If the readiness check fails, your service is marked as not ready. Note that your service can be healthy, but not necessarily ready to receive requests. A readiness check looks similar to the liveness probe:

```
readinessProbe:
  httpGet:
    path: /alive
    port: 8080
  initialDelaySeconds: 5
  timeoutSeconds: 1
  periodSeconds: 15
```

Just like with the liveness probe, you define the endpoint and the port to which the platform can make requests. With the previous snippet, the platform waits for 5 seconds before calling the endpoint and then repeats the call every 15 seconds. In addition, you also defined a timeout, so if the service doesn't respond in 1 second, it's deemed as not ready. If the service is not ready, Kubernetes marks it as such, and none of the requests through the Kubernetes service will be routed to the unready pod.

Configuration Management

Most services and functions don't live in isolation, and they always need to be able to communicate with other services and systems. One of the factors from the Twelve-Factor manifesto (*https://12factor.net/*) talks about configuration and specifies storing configuration in the environment.

Service or function configuration contains everything your service or function needs to be able to start up and run. Some of the common configuration settings the app needs are:

- Database/queue/messaging connection strings
- Credentials (usernames, passwords, API keys, certificates)
- Timeouts, ports, dependent service names

The Twelve-Factor manifesto mentions that code and configuration should be strictly separated, which makes your service easily configurable for different environments. If you are unsure what should be part of the configuration, a good guideline is to make something configurable only if it can change between deployments. With this guideline in mind, settings like timeouts are considered service settings and are not part of the service configuration. When developing your services, design them in such a way that you can easily add new configuration settings or remove them without breaking things.

Sometimes, handling environment variables and knowing which variables are required for each service can become difficult. You can decide to group your environment variables per environment (staging, testing, production) or even per deployment (if they change) and store them in separate configuration files. For example, you can create a configuration file called *production.yaml* and *staging.yaml*—both files would contain the same setting and environment variables names, but the values would be specific to that environment only. If you decide to go this way, design your service so that it can read configuration from an external file. It's also recommended that you come up with a strict configuration schema that all configuration files need to follow. With a strict schema in place, the configuration testing becomes much easier.

A common way to store configuration settings in Kuberentes is using a resource called ConfigMap. The ConfigMap allows for great separation of configuration from the services, which makes your service more portable.

Each ConfigMap has a unique name and a data source. The data source can be one of these three things:

- Directory
- File
- Literal value

To create a ConfigMap from a directory, you can use the Kuberetes CLI:

```
kubectl create configmap my-svc-config --from-file=my-service/config-files/
```

This command takes all files in the */my-service/config-files/* folder and combines them into a single ConfigMap resource. You can use the same Kubernetes CLI command to create a ConfigMap from a single file, but instead of pointing to a folder, you would point the `--from-file` argument to a single file.

Another common way of describing and storing environment variables is by using an environment file. In the environment file, you define the environment variable names in the format `"NAME=VALUE"` and store it in a file:

username=user

password=mypassword

With the `--from-env-file` option in the Kuberentes CLI, you can use your existing environment files and generate Kuberentes ConfigMaps like this:

```
kubectl create configmap my-env-file --from-env-file=production.env
```

This command takes the *production.env* environment file and creates a ConfigMap named *my-env-file* that looks like this:

```
apiVersion: v1
data:
  password: pwd
  username: user
kind: ConfigMap
metadata:
  creationTimestamp: 2019-02-08T18:57:29Z
  name: my-env-file
  namespace: default
  resourceVersion: "284220"
  selfLink: /api/v1/namespaces/default/configmaps/my-env-file
  uid: 623618bd-2bd3-11e9-b554-025000000001
```

However, if you want to create a ConfigMap from a single value only, you can use the `--from-literal` setting. The created ConfigMap would look very similar to the one shown.

Now that you have the ConfigMaps defined, you can use them within your pods in multiple different ways.

Single-Environment Variable

You can mount the values stored in a ConfigMap as environment variables in your pods using a snippet where you define an environment variable name (MY_USERNAME), the ConfigMap name (my-env-file), and the key within the ConfigMap (username) that contains the value you want to assign to the environment variable. This option is useful if you are using one-off environment variables:

```
env:
  - name: MY_USERNAME
    valueFrom:
     configMapKeyRef:
       name: my-env-file
       key: username
```

Multiple-Environment Variables

When you have a ConfigMap with multiple values defined, you can use a key named envFrom to declare all values from the ConfigMap as environment variables within your pod:

```
envFrom:
  -configMapKeyRef:
    name: my-env-file
```

Using the ConfigMap with username and password we deployed earlier, this snippet would create two environment variables called username and password within your pod.

Adding ConfigMap Data to a Volume

If you created a ConfigMap from a file or directory, you use a volume that will add all data in the ConfigMap to the directory of your choosing within the pod:

```
volumeMounts:
  - name: config-volume
    mountPath: /etc/config
...
volumes:
  - name:   config-volume
    configMap:
      name: my-config-files
```

In your pod definition, you are declaring a volume called config-volume that contains all files from the my-config-files ConfigMap. In the container definition, you are mounting that volume by referring to it by name and specifying the mount path *etc/config*. With this definition, you can access the *etc/config* folder within your service to read any of the configuration files defined in the ConfigMap.

A nice thing about using ConfigMaps and mounting them within pods is that they also are refreshed and updated automatically. If you need to update only your configuration, you can, and Kubernetes ensures that the values are updated within your pods as well.

Storing Secrets

Not all configuration settings are equal. The values such as port numbers and service names usually don't require any special treatment in terms of securing them or making sure that they don't leak or are logged anywhere. However, passwords, API keys, and certificates can be a bit more delicate.

The Kubernetes platform has a dedicated resource called Secret that you can use to deal with these types of configuration values. Instead of taking a password and putting it directly into the pod definition, you store it in a separate secret resource and then you mount that resource to your pod. These secret resources then can be managed entirely separately from other resources. By default, secrets in Kubernetes are stored in the *etcd* instance. When running your services in production, consider using one of the secret management solutions, such as Vault by HashiCorp.

Within each secret, you could store multiple secret values that are base64-encoded and create a YAML file that contains the secret:

```
apiVersion: v1
kind: Secret
metadata:
  name: mongodb
  type: Opaque
  data:
    username: dXNlcm5hbWUK
    password: SUxvdmVVQaXp6YQo=
```

Alternatively, you could use Kubernetes CLI to create the secret resource like this:

```
kubectl create secret generic mongodb \
        --from-literal=username=user \
        --from-literal=password=pwd
```

Instead of declaring each value separately, you can also use a file and then store the entire file in a secret. With secrets in place, you can mount them as environment variables within your pods this way:

```
env:
- name: USERNAME
  valueFrom:
    secretKeyRef:
      name: mongodb-secrets
```

```
        key: username
  - name: PASSWORD
    valueFrom:
      secretKeyRef:
        name: mongodb-secrets
        key: password
```

When the pod starts, Kubernetes ensures that the secret is read and environment variable values are created based on the values stored in the secret resource. One thing to keep in mind when consuming secrets as environment variables is to ensure that you are not logging the environment variables as part of the service startup: in the event that the service fails, you might expose secrets. If possible, try to consume secrets from files instead.

A simplest way for storing secrets and configuration settings for functions is to add them to the function configuration/environment. However, this is not necessarily the best practice. A better approach is to use one of the managed solutions from the cloud provider where your functions are running. Both AWS Lambda and Azure Functions are integrated with their respective configuration management solutions. In AWS, you can use the systems manager parameter store, and in Azure you can use Key Vault. Both managed services provide a secure storage for configuration data management and secret management. You can store passwords, connection strings, certificates, and other configuration settings in a central place. Instead of storing secrets as settings for each function, you have the ability to programmatically retrieve the values from the managed services.

Deployment Configuration

Until now, we've talked about service and application configuration management. Let's try to see how you can manage the configuration of your deployments.

One of the popular tools with the Kubernetes platform, Helm (*https://helm.sh*), is used to define so-called *charts* (a collection of templatized Kubernetes resource files) that you can install and upgrade. Charts allow you to package multiple Kubernetes resource files together and then manage, install, and upgrade them as a single unit. The resource files can be templatized and include template values that are defined in a separate file (usually called *values.yaml*).

Take, for example, this snippet from a Kubernetes deployment resource:

```
containers:
- image: serviceregistry/hellosvc:1.0.0
  imagePullPolicy: Always
  name: web
  ports:
  - containerPort: 8080
  env:
  - name: PORT
```

```
      value: "8080"
    - name: METRICS_PORT
      value: "9090"
    - name: DB_CONN_STRING
      value: "mongodb://user:pwd@mongo.com:27017/admin"
```

Here, we are declaring three environment variables in the previous snippet: two ports and the database connection string. Ports will likely not change if you are doing deployments to different environments; however, the possibility of database connection string being different is much higher. There's also the image name that changes with every deployment. With the help of Helm, you could templatize those values, and the snippet would like something like this:

```
containers:
- image: "{{ .Values.hellosvc.imageName }}"
  imagePullPolicy: Always
  name: web              .
  ports:
  - containerPort: "{{ .Values.hellosvc.port}}"
  env:
  - name: PORT
    value: "{{ .Values.hellosvc.port}}"
    - name: METRICS_PORT
      value: "{{ .Values.hellosvc.metricsPort }}"
    - name: DB_CONN_STRING
      value: "{{ .Values.hellosvc.dbConnString }}"
```

We are using curly braces to define a template that is replaced with an actual value after you use Helm to install or upgrade the chart. This is how the *values.yaml* file would look with the templatized variables defined:

```
hellosvc:
  imageName: serviceregistry/hellosvc:1.0.0
  port: 8080
  metricsPort: 9090
  dbConnString: "mongodb://user:pwd@mongo.com:27017/admin"
```

Similarly, you could create a separate file that holds different values and then use the Helm CLI to install the chart like this:

```
helm install -f my-values.yaml ./myChart
```

By default, Helm uses the *values.yaml* file, and you can overwrite certain variables with the following syntax:

```
helm install -set PORT=1234 ./myChart
```

You can probably already see the flexibility of using templatized deployment files. Tools like Helm can also help you to automate deployment file creation within your Continuous Deployment process easily. Another useful command in the Helm CLI is the one that allows you to apply values to the template files and generate the output files without actually deploying them. In addition to the built-in Helm command for

---

validating the charts, the outputted template files then can be fed as an input to configuration testing if needed.

For packaging a composite cloud native application using multiple config-as-code tools and configuration scripts for the app itself, you can use the cloud native application bundle (CNAB (*https://cnab.io*)). You can compose the bundle to use any infrastructure or services your application needs, without locking you into any specific cloud vendor. Additionally, the bundles are signed and verified. This is a way that you can get a cloud native application into an air-gapped environment.

Sample CI/CD Flows

Considering all of the approaches and techniques described in this chapter, you could come up with a more detailed code flow for containerized applications that would be similar to the one in Figure 5-10.

Note that Figure 5-10 is just a guideline, representing one way you could do your deployments and releases. There is an infinite number of different requirements that could significantly change how your actual process looks and works. Here are all the steps in the flow with corresponding descriptions:

1. Code complete: the code was written.
2. Push to Git: code is committed and pushed to the code repository.
3. Pull code: the build system pulls the latest pushed code.
4. Source code analysis: static code analysis is run on the source code.
5. Build container: source code is built, copied, and packaged into a container.
6. Unit/service tests: unit and service tests are run. If the tests fail, the CI fails and flow is stopped.
7. Push to private registry: built and tested image is tagged and pushed to the private registry.
8. Image security scanning: any image that's pushed to the registry is scanned for potential vulnerabilities and exploits.
9. Test configuration: before deploying containers to an environment, the configuration tests are run. On failure, the flow stops.

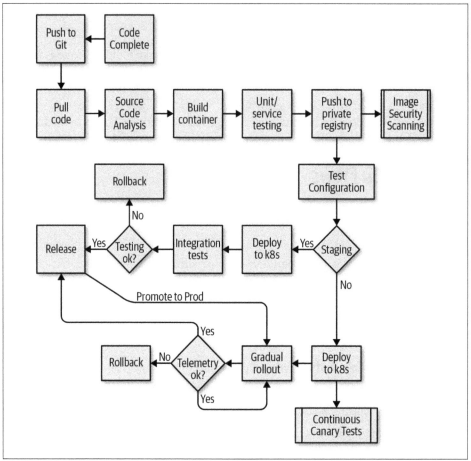

Figure 5-10. Sample CI/CD flow

If deploying to staging:

1. Deploy to k8s: published container is deployed to Kubernetes.

2. Integration tests: integration tests are executed.

3. Rollback: if integration tests fail, deployment is rolled back and the flow stops.

4. Release: if integration tests pass, deployment gets released and is available in the staging environment.

5. Promotion to Prod: when ready, the changes are promoted to the production environment using gradual rollout.

If deploying to production:

1. Deploy to k8s: published container is deployed to Kubernetes.
2. Continuous canary tests: a set of tests continuously run to catch potential issues as soon as possible.
3. Gradual rollout: amount of traffic is being gradually increased (i.e., more and more traffic is sent to the deployed version).
4. Telemetry: continuously monitor telemetry to ensure gradual rollout is working correctly and no issues are introduced with the deployment. If we see failures through telemetry, the changes are rolled back; otherwise, more traffic is routed to the deployed version.
5. Release: as soon as 100% of the traffic is flowing to the deployed version, the release is completed.

Similarly, Figure 5-11 shows how a sample CI/CD flow for serverless applications would look.

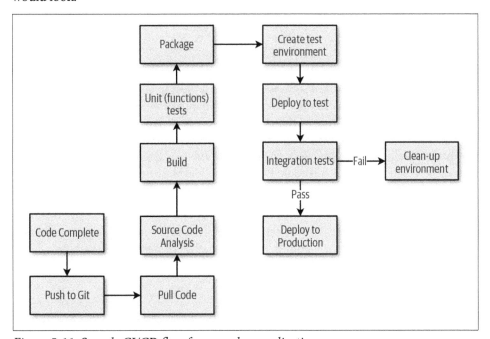

Figure 5-11. Sample CI/CD flow for serverless applications

1. Code complete: the code was written.
2. Push to Git: code is committed and pushed to the code repository.
3. Pull code: the build system pulls the latest pushed code.

4. Source code analysis: static code analysis is run on the source code.

5. Build: functions source code gets built.

6. Unit (functions) tests: unit and functions tests are run. If the tests fail, the CI fails and flow is stopped.

7. Package: code gets packaged (as a ZIP file, for example).

8. Create test environment: test environment is created using a template such as AWS SAM.

9. Deploy to test: packaged serverless application and any dependencies are deployed to the test environment.

10. Integration tests: integration tests are executed.

11. Clean-up environment: test environment is torn down and deleted if integration tests fail.

12. Deploy to Production: if integration tests pass, serverless application is deployed to production. Any test environments and other dependencies created by the flow are removed. This concludes the flow.

Summary

In this chapter, we looked at the fundamentals of DevOps, its values, and practical examples on how to measure the organization's maturity. We gave a broad overview of what it means to do testing in the cloud native world. We explained various types of tests that you should consider and when you should execute those tests. The testing in the production section took you through the process of getting to a point in your organization at which you could begin doing your testing in production.

To help you get to that point, we described multiple different tools that you could use, how to set up your development environment (be it a local development environment or cloud environment), and how to get started with monitoring, tracing, and dealing with service and deployment configuration. Finally, we described example CI/CD flows for containerized services and serverless applications.

CHAPTER 6

Best Practices

Throughout this book, you have learned about the fundamentals of cloud native applications—how to design, develop, and operate them as well as how to deal with data. To conclude, this chapter aims to provide a laundry list covering tips, proven techniques, and proven best practices to build and manage reactive cloud native applications.

Moving to Cloud Native

In Chapter 2, you learned about the process that many customers follow when moving traditional applications to the cloud. There are many best practices and lessons learned that you should consider when moving an existing application into the cloud.

Breaking Up the Monolith for the Right Reasons

"Never change a running system" is a widely used statement in software development, and it is also applicable when you consider moving your application to the cloud. If your sole requirement is to move your application to the cloud, you can always consider moving it on Infrastructure as a Service (IaaS)—in fact, that should be your very first step. That said, there are benefits of redesigning your application to be cloud native, but you need to weigh the pros and cons. Following are some guidelines indicating that a redesign makes sense:

- Your codebase has grown to a point that it takes very long to release an updated version and thus you cannot react to new market or customer requirements quickly.

- Components of your applications have different scale requirements. A good example is a traditional three-tier application consisting of a frontend, business, and data tier. Only the frontend tier might experience heavy load in user requests, whereas the business and data tier are still comfortably handling the load. As mentioned in Chapter 2 and Chapter 3, cloud native applications allow you to scale services independently.

- Better technology choices have emerged. There is constant innovation in the technology sector, and some new technologies might be better suited for parts of your application.

After you have decided that you want to redesign your application, you need to consider many things. In the following sections, we provide a comprehensive look at these considerations.

Decouple Simple Services First

Start by breaking off components that provide simpler functionality because they usually do not have a lot of dependencies and, thus, are not deeply integrated within the monolith.

Learn to Operate on a Small Scale

Use the first service as a learning path for how to operate in a cloud native world. Starting with a simple service, you can focus on setting up automation to provision the infrastructure and the CI/CD pipeline so that you become familiar with the process of developing, deploying, and operating a cloud native service. Having a simple service and minimal infrastructure will allow you to learn, exercise, and improve your new process ahead of time, without substantial impact on the monolith and your end users.

Use an Anticorruption Layer Pattern

Nothing is perfect, especially in the software development world, so you will eventually end up with a new service that makes calls back to the monolith. In this case, you might want to use the *Anticorruption Layer* pattern. This pattern is used to implement a facade or adapter between components that don't share the same semantics. The purpose of the anticorruption layer is to translate the request from one component to another; for example, implementing protocol or schema translations.

To implement this, you design and create a new API in the monolith that makes calls through the anticorruption layer in the new service, as shown in Figure 6-1.

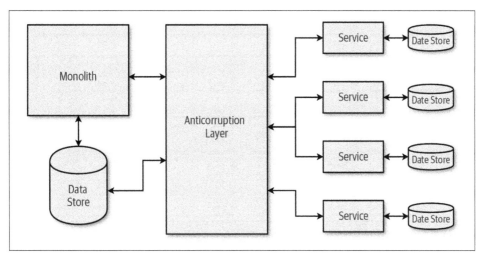

Figure 6-1. Anticorruption Layer pattern

There are a couple of considerations when you are using this approach. As Figure 6-1 illustrates, the anticorruption layer is a service on its own, so you need to think about how to scale and operate the layer. Also, you need to think about whether you want to retire the anticorruption layer after the monolithic application has been fully moved into a cloud native application.

Use a Strangler Pattern

When you are decomposing your monolith to move to microservices and functions, you can use a gateway and a pattern such as a *Strangler* pattern. The idea behind the Strangler pattern is to use the gateway as a facade while you gradually move the back-end monolith to a new architecture—either services, functions, or a combination of both. As you're making progress breaking up the monolith and implementing those pieces of functionality as services or functions, you update the gateway to redirect requests to the new functionality, instead as shown in Figure 6-2.

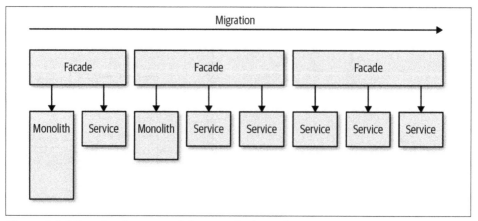

Figure 6-2. Migrating from monolith using the Strangler pattern

Note that the Strangler pattern might not be suitable for the instance in which you can't intercept the requests going to the backing monolith. The pattern also might not make sense if you have a smaller system, for which it's easier and faster to replace the entire system, instead of gradually moving it.

The Anticorruption Layer and Strangler patterns have been proven many times as good approaches to move a monolithic legacy application to a cloud native application because both promote a gradual approach.

Come Up with a Data Migration Strategy

In a monolith, you are usually working with a centrally shared datastore where data is read from and written to by multiple places and services. To truly move to the cloud native architecture, you need to decouple data as well. Your data migration strategy might consist of multiple phases, especially if you can't migrate everything at the same time. However, in most cases, you will need to do an incremental migration while keeping the entire system running. A gradual migration will probably involve writing data twice (to the new and old datastore) for a while. After you have data in both places and synchronized, you will need to modify where the data is being read from and then read everything from the new store. Finally, you should be able to stop writing data to the old store completely.

Rewrite Any Boilerplate Code

Monoliths will usually have large amounts of code that deals with the configuration, data caching, datastore access, and so on and is probably using older libraries and frameworks. When moving capabilities to a new service, you should rewrite this code. The best option is to throw away the old code and rewrite it from scratch instead of modifying the existing code and molding it so it fits the new service.

Reconsider Frameworks, Languages, Data Structures, and Datastores

Moving to microservices gives you an option to rethink the existing implementation. Are there new frameworks or languages that you could use to rewrite the current code that provide better features and functionalities for your scenarios? If it makes sense to rewrite the code, do it! Also, reconsider any data structures in the current code. Would they still make sense when moved to a service? You should also evaluate whether you want to use different datastores. Chapter 4 outlines what datastores are best suited for certain data structures and query patterns.

Retire Code

After you've created a new service and all the traffic is redirected to that service, you need to retire and remove the old code that resides in the monolith. Using this approach, you are shrinking the monolith and expanding your services.

Ensuring Resiliency

Resiliency is the ability of a system to recover from failures and continue to function and serve requests. Resiliency is not about avoiding failures; instead, it is all about responding to failures in such a manner that avoids significant downtime or data loss.

Handle Transient Failures with Retries

Requests can fail due to multiple reasons such as network latency, dropped connections, or timeouts if downstream services are busy. You can avoid most of these failures if you retry the request. Retrying can also improve the stability of your application. However, before blindly retrying all requests, you need to implement a bit of logic that determines whether the request should be retried. If the failure is not transient or there is a likelihood that a retry won't be successful, it is better for the component to cancel the request and respond with an appropriate error message. For example, retrying a failed login because of an incorrect password is futile and retries won't help. If failure is due to a rare network issue, you can retry the request right away given that the same issue probably won't persist. Finally, if the failure happens because the downstream service is busy or you are being rate limited, for example, you should retry after a delay. Here are some common strategies for delaying between retry operations:

Constant
   Wait for the same time between each attempt.

Linear
   Incrementally increase the time between each retry. For example, you can start with one second, then three seconds, five seconds, and so on.

Exponential back-off
> Exponentially increase time between each retry. For example, start with 3 seconds, 12 seconds, 30 seconds, and so on.

Depending on what type of failure you are dealing with, you can also immediately retry the operation once and then use one of the delay strategies mentioned in the preceding list. You can handle retries in the component's source code by using the retry and transient failure logic provided by many of the service SDKs, or at the infrastructure layer if you are using a service mesh, such as Istio.

Use a Finite Number of Retries

Regardless of which retry strategy you're using, always make sure to use a finite number of retries. Having an infinite number of retries will cause an unnecessary strain on the system.

Use Circuit Breakers for Nontransient Failures

The purpose of a circuit breaker is to prevent components from doing operations that will likely fail and are not transient. Circuit breakers monitor the number of faults, and based on that information decide whether the request should continue or an error should be returned without even invoking the downstream service. If a circuit breaker trips, the number of failures has exceeded a predefined value, and the circuit breaker will automatically return errors for a preset time. After the preset time elapses, it will reset the failure count and allow requests to go through to the downstream service again. A well-known library that implements the circuit breaker pattern is Hystrix from Netflix. If you are using a service mesh like Istio or Envoy proxies, you can take advantage of the circuit breaker implementation in those solutions.

Graceful Degradation

Services should degrade gracefully, so even if they fail, they still provide an acceptable user experience if it makes sense. For example, if you can't retrieve the data, you could display a cached version of the data, and as soon as the data source recovers, you show the latest data.

Use a Bulkhead Pattern

The *Bulkhead* pattern refers to isolating different parts of your system into groups in such a way that if one fails, the others will continue running unaffected. Grouping your services this way allows you isolate failures and continue serving requests even when there's a failure.

Implement Health Checks and Readiness Checks

Implement a health check and a readiness check for every service you deploy. The platform can use these to determine whether the service is healthy and performing correctly as well as when the service is ready to start accepting requests. In Kubernetes, health checks are called *probes*. The liveness probe is used to determine when a container should be restarted, whereas the readiness probe determines whether a pod should start receiving traffic.

The initial delay defines the number of seconds after the container has started before liveness or readiness probes are active, whereas the period defines how often the probe is performed. There are also additional settings such as success/failure threshold and timeouts that you can use to fine-tune the probes.

Define CPU and Memory Limits for Your Containers

You should define CPU and memory limits to isolate resources and prevent certain services instances from consuming too many resources. In Kubernetes, you can achieve this by defining the memory and CPU limits within the pod definition.

Implement Rate Limiting and Throttling

You use rate limiting and throttling to limit the number of incoming or outgoing requests for a service. Implementing those can help you to keep your service responsive even in the case of a sudden spike in requests. Throttling, on the other hand, is often used for outgoing requests. Think about using it when you want to control the number of requests sent to an external service to minimize the costs or to make sure that your service does not look like the origin of a Denial-of-Service attack.

Ensuring Security

Security in the cloud native world is based on the shared responsibility model. The cloud providers are not solely responsible for the security of their customers' solutions; instead, they share that responsibility with the customers. From an application perspective you should consider adopting the defense-in-depth concept, which is discussed in Chapter 3. The best practices listed in this section will help you to ensure security.

Treat Security Requirements the Same as Any Other Requirements

Having fully automated processes is in spirit of the cloud native development. To achieve this, all security requirements must be treated as any other requirement and be pushed through your development pipeline.

Incorporate Security in Your Designs

As you're planning and designing your cloud native solutions, you need to think about security and incorporate the security features in your design. As part of your design, you also should call out any additional security concerns that need to be addressed during component development.

Grant Least-Privileged Access

If your services or functions need access to any resources, they should be granted specific permissions that have the least amount of access set to them. For example, if your service is reading only from the database, it does not need to use an account that has write permissions.

Use Separate Accounts/Subscriptions/Tenants

Depending on the terminology of your cloud provider, your cloud native system should use separate accounts, subscriptions, and/or tenants. At the very least, you will need a separate account for every environment you will be using; that way, you can ensure proper isolation between environments.

Securely Store All Secrets

Any secrets within your system, used either by your components or Continuous Integration/Continuous Development (CI/CD) pipeline, need to be encrypted and securely stored. It might sound like a no-brainer, but never store any secrets in plain text: always encrypt them. It's always best to use existing and proven secret management systems that take care of these things for you. The simplest option is to use Kubernetes Secrets to store the secrets used by services within the cluster. Secrets are stored in etcd, a distributed key/value store. However, managed and centralized solutions have multiple advantages over Kubernetes secrets: everything is stored in a centralized location, you can define access control policies, secrets are encrypted, auditing support is provided, and more. Some examples of managed solutions are Microsoft Azure Key Vault, Amazon Secrets Manager, and HashiCorp Vault.

Obfuscate Data

Any data your component uses needs to be properly obfuscated. For example, you never want to log any data classified as Personally Identifiable Information (PII) in plain text; if you need to log or store it, ensure that it's either obfuscated (if logging it) or encrypted (if storing it).

Encrypt Data in Transit

Encrypting data in transit protects your data if communications are intercepted while the data moves between components. To achieve this protection, you need to encrypt the data before transmitting it, authenticate the endpoints, and finally decrypt and verify the data after it reaches the endpoint. Transport Layer Security (TLS) is used to encrypt data in transit for transport security. If you are using a service mesh, TLS might already be implemented between the proxies in the mesh.

Use Federated Identity Management

Using an existing federated identity management service (Auth0, for example) to handle how users sign up, sign in, and sign out allows you to redirect users to a third-party page for authentication. Your component should delegate authentication and authorization whenever possible.

Use Role-Based Access Control

Role-Based Access Control (RBAC) has been around for a long time. RBAC is a control access mechanism around roles and privileges, and as you have learned, it can be a great asset to your defense-in-depth strategy because it allows you to provide fine-grained access to users to only the resources they need. Kubernetes RBAC, for example, controls permissions to the Kubernetes API. Using RBAC, you can allow or deny specific users from creating deployments or listing pods, and more. It's a good practice to scope Kubernetes RBAC permissions by namespaces rather than cluster roles.

Isolate Kubernetes Pods

Any pods running in a Kubernetes cluster are not isolated and can accept requests from any source. Defining a network policy on pods allows you to isolate pods and make them reject any connections that are not allowed by the policy. For example, if a component in your system is compromised, a network policy will prevent the malicious actor from communicating with services with which you don't want them to communicate. Using a NetworkPolicy resource in Kubernetes, you can define a pod selector and detailed ingress and egress policies.

Working with Data

Most modern applications have some need to store and work with data. A growing number of data storage and analytics services are available as cloud provider–managed services. Cloud native applications are designed to take full advantage of cloud provider–managed data systems and are designed to evolve to take advantage of a growing number of features. When working with data in the cloud, many of the standard data best practices still apply: have a disaster recovery plan, keep business logic out of the database, avoid overfetching or excessively chatty I/O, use data access implementations that prevent SQL injections attacks, and so on.

Use Managed Databases and Analytics Services

Whenever possible use a managed database. Provisioning a database on virtual machines (VMs) or in a Kubernetes cluster can often be a quick and easy task. Production databases that require backups and replicas can quickly increase the time and burden of operating data storage systems. By offloading the operational burden of deploying and managing a database, teams are able to focus more on development.

In some cases, a data storage technology might not be available as a managed service or it might be necessary to have access to some configurations that are not available in a managed version of the system.

Use a Datastore That Best Fits Data Requirements

When designing on-premises applications, architects would often try to avoid using multiple databases. Each database technology used would require database administrators with the skillset to deploy and manage the database, significantly increasing the operational costs of the application. The reduced operational costs of cloud-managed databases make it possible to use multiple different types of datastores to put data in a system best suited for the data type, read, and write requirements. Cloud native applications take full advantage of this, using multiple data storage technologies.

Keep Data in Multiple Regions or Zones

Store production data for applications across multiple regions or zones. How the data is stored across the zones or regions will depend on the application's availability requirements; for example, the data might be backups or a replicated database. If a cloud provider experiences a failure of a zone or region, the data can be available to be used for recovery or failover.

Use Data Partitioning and Replication for Scale

Cloud native applications are designed to scale out as opposed to scale up. Scaling a database up is achieved by increasing the resources available to a database instance; for example, adding more cores or memory. This ultimately encounters a hard limit and can be costly. Scaling databases out is achieved through distributing the data across multiple instances of a database. The database is partitioned, or broken up, and stored in multiple databases.

Avoid Overfetching and Chatty I/O

Overfetching is when an application requests data from a database but needs only a fraction of the data for the operation. For example, an application might display a list of orders with a simple summary but request the entire order and order details without needing it. A chatty application, on the other hand, makes a lot of small calls to complete an operation when a single request can be made to the database.

Don't Put Business Logic in the Database

Too many application scaling issues are the result of putting too much logic in the database. Databases made it easy to put business logic inside the database by supporting standard development languages, and it became convenient to perform these tasks in the database. This often introduces scaling issues because a database is commonly an expensive shared resource.

Test with Production-like Data

Create automation to anonymize production data that can be updated with new rules as the data changes. Applications should be tested with production-like data. Data is sometimes pulled from production systems, scrubbed, and loaded into test systems to provide production-like data. You should automate this process so that it is easy to update as the data changes.

Handle Transient Failures

As mentioned in the resiliency section of this chapter, failures will happen. Expect failures when making calls to a database and be prepared to handle them. Many of the database client libraries support transient fault handling already. It's important to understand whether they do and how it's supported.

Performance and Scalability

Performance indicates how well a system can execute an operation within a certain time frame, whereas scalability refers to how a system can handle load increase without impact on the performance. Predicting periods of increased activity to a system can be tough, so the components need to be able to scale out as needed to meet the increased demand and then scale down, after the demand decreases. The subsections that follow present some best practices to help you achieve optimal performance and scalability.

Design Stateless Services That Scale Out

Services should be designed to scale out. Scaling out is an approach to increasing the scale of a service by adding more instances of a service. Scaling up is an approach to scaling a service by adding more resources like memory or cores, but this method generally has a hard limit. By designing a service to scale out and back in, you can scale the service to handle variations in the load without impacting the availability of the service.

Stateful applications are inherently difficult to scale and should be avoided. If stateful services are necessary, it's generally best to separate the functionality from the application and use a partitioning strategy and managed services if they are available.

Use Platform Autoscaling Features

When possible, use any autoscaling features that are built into the platform before implementing your own. Kubernetes offers Horizontal Pod Autoscaler (HPA). HPA scales the pods based on the CPU, memory, or custom metrics. You specify the metric (e.g., 85% of CPU or 16 GB of memory) and the minimum and maximum number of pod replicas. After the target metric is reached, Kubernetes automatically scales the pods. Similarly, cluster autoscaling scales the number of cluster nodes if pods can't be scheduled. Cluster autoscaling uses the requested resources in the pod specification to determine whether nodes should be added.

Use Caching

Caching is a technique that can help improve the performance of your component by temporarily storing frequently used data in storage that's close to the component. This improves the response time because the component does not need to go to the original source. The most basic type of cache is an in-memory store that is being used by a single process. If you have multiple instances of your component, each instance will have its own independent copy of the in-memory cache. This can cause consistency problems if data is not static because the different instances will have different versions of cached data. To solve this problem, you can use shared caching, which ensures that different component instances use the same cached data. In this case, cache is stored separately, usually in front of the database.

Use Partitioning to Scale Beyond Service Limits

Cloud services will often have some defined scale limits. It's important to understand the scalability limits of each of the services used and how much they can be scaled up. If a single service is unable to scale to meet the application's requirements, create multiple service instances and partition work across the instances. For example, if a managed gateway was capable of handling 80% of the application's intended load, create another gateway and split the services across the gateway.

Functions

Much of the software development life cycle (SDLC) and general server architecture best practices are the same for serverless architectures. Given serverless is a different operating model, there are, however, some best practices specific to functions.

Write Single-Purpose Functions

Follow the single-responsibility principle and only write functions that have a single responsibility. This will make your functions easier to reason about, test, and, when the time comes, debug.

Don't Chain Functions

In general, functions should push messages/data to a queue or a datastore to trigger any other functions if needed. Having one or more functions call other functions is often considered an antipattern that additionally increases your cost and makes the debugging more difficult. If your application requires the daisy-chaining of functions, you should consider using function offerings such as Azure Durable Functions or AWS Step Functions.

Keep Functions Light and Simple

Each function should do just one thing and rely on only a minimal number of external libraries. Any extra and unnecessary code in the function makes the function bigger in size, and that affects the start time.

Make Functions Stateless

Don't save any data in your functions because new function instances usually run in their own isolated environment and don't share anything with other functions or invocations of the same function.

Separate Function Entry Point from the Function Logic

Functions will have an entry point invoked by the function framework. Framework-specific context is generally passed to the function entry point, along with invocation context. For example, if the function is invoked through an HTTP request like an API gateway, the context will contain HTTP-specific details. The entry-point method should separate these entry-point details from the rest of the code. This will improve manageability, testability, and portability of the functions.

Avoid Long-Running Functions

Most Function as a Service (FaaS) offerings have an upper limit for execution time per function. As a result, long-running functions can cause issues such as increased load times and timeouts. Whenever possible, refactor large functions into smaller ones that work together.

Use Queues for Cross-Function Communication

Instead of passing information among one another, functions should use a queue to which to post the messages. Other functions can be triggered and executed based off the events that happen on that queue (item added, removed, updated, etc.).

Operations

A DevOps practice provides the foundation necessary for organizations to make the best use of cloud technologies. Cloud native applications utilize DevOps principles and best practices that are detailed in Chapter 5.

Deployments and Releases Are Separate Activities

It is important to make a distinction between deployment and release. Deployment is the act of taking the built component and placing it within an environment—the component is fully configured and ready to go; however, there is no traffic being sent to it. As part of the component release, we begin to allow traffic to the deployed component. This separation allows you to do gradual releases, A/B testing, and canary deployments in a controlled manner.

Keep Deployments Small

Each component deployment should be a small event that can be performed by a single team in a short time. There is no general rule about how small a deployment should be and how much time it should take to deploy a component, because this is highly dependent on the component, your process, and the change to the component. A good approach is to be able to roll out a critical fix within a day.

CI/CD Definition Lives with the Component

You need to store and version any CI/CD configuration and dependencies alongside the component. Each push to the component's branch triggers the pipeline and executes jobs defined in the CI/CD configuration. To control component deployments to different environments (development, staging, production), you can use the Git branch names and configure your pipeline to deploy the master branch only to a production environment, for example.

Consistent Application Deployment

With a consistently reliable and repeatable deployment process, you can minimize errors. Automate as many processes as possible and ensure that you have a rollback plan defined in case deployment fails.

Use Zero-Downtime Releases

To maximize the availability of your system during releases, consider using zero-downtime releases such as blue/green or canary. Using one of these approaches also allows you to quickly roll back the update in case of failures.

Don't Modify Deployed Infrastructure

Infrastructure should be immutable. Modifying deployed infrastructure can quickly get out of hand, and keeping track of what changed can be complicated. If you need to update the infrastructure, redeploy it instead.

Use Containerized Build

To avoid configuring build environments, package your build process into Docker containers. Consider using multiple images and containers for builds instead of creating a single, monolithic build image.

Describe Infrastructure Using Code

Infrastructure should be described using either cloud provider's declarative templates or a programming language or scripts that provision the infrastructure.

Use Namespaces to Organize Services in Kubernetes

Every resource in a Kubernetes cluster belongs to a namespace. By default, newly created resources go into a namespace called *default*. For better organization of services, it is a good practice to use descriptive names and group services into bounded contexts.

Isolate the Environments

Use a dedicated production cluster and physically separate the production cluster for your development, staging, or testing environments.

Separate Function Source Code

Each function must be independently versioned and have its own dependencies. If that's not the case, you will end up with a monolith and a tightly coupled codebase.

Correlate Deployments with Commits

Pick a branching strategy that allows you to correlate the deployments to specific commits in your branch and that also allows you to identify which version of the source code is deployed.

Logging, Monitoring, and Alerting

Application and infrastructure logging can provide much more value than just root-cause analysis. A proper logging solution will provide valuable insights into applications and systems, and it's often necessary for monitoring the health of an application and alerting operations of important events. As cloud applications become more distributed, logging and instrumentation become increasingly challenging and important.

Use a Unified Logging System

Use a unified logging system capable of capturing log messages across all services and levels of a system and store them in a centralized store. Whether you move all logs to a centralized store for analysis and search, or you leave them on the machine with the necessary tools in place to run a distributed query, it's important that an engineer can find and analyze logs without having to go from one system to the next.

Use Correlation IDs

Include a unique correlation ID (CID) that is passed through all services. If one of the services fails, the correlation ID is used to trace the request through the system and pinpoint where the failure occurred.

Include Context with Log Entries

Each log entry should contain additional context that can help when you are investigating issues. For example, include all exception handling, retry attempts, service name or ID, image version, binary version, and so on.

Common and Structured Logging Format

Decide on a common and structured logging format that all components will use. This will allow you to quickly search and parse the logs later on. Also, make sure you are using the same time zone information in all your components. In general, it is best to adhere to a common time format such as Coordinated Universal Time (UTC).

Tag Your Metrics Appropriately

In addition to using clear and unique metric names, make sure that you are storing any additional information, such as component name, environment, function name, region, and so forth, in the metric tags. With tags in place, you can create queries, dashboards, and reports using multiple dimensions (e.g., average latency across a specific region or across regions for a specific function).

Avoid Alert Fatigue

The sheer number of metrics makes it difficult to determine how to set up the alerting and what to alert on. If you are firing off too many alerts, eventually people will stop paying attention to them and no longer take them seriously. Also, investigating a bunch of alerts can become overwhelming and it could be the only thing your team is doing. It is important to classify alerts by severity: low, moderate, and high. The purpose of low-severity alerts is to potentially use them later, when doing root-cause analysis of a high-severity alert. You can use them to uncover certain patterns, but they do not require any immediate action when fired. A moderate-severity alert should either create a notification or open a ticket. These are the alerts you want to look at, but are not high priority and don't need immediate action. They could represent a temporary condition (increase demand, for example) that eventually goes away. They also give you an early warning of a possible high-severity alert. Finally, high-severity alerts are the ones that will wake people up in the middle of the night and require immediate action. Recently, machine learning–based approaches to automatically triage issues and raise alerts are gaining in popularity, and the term AIOps has even been introduced.

Define and Alert on Key Performance Indicators

Cloud native systems will have a plethora of signals that are being emitted and monitored. You need to filter down those signals and determine which ones are the most important and valuable. These Key Performance Indicators (KPIs) give you insight into the health of your system. For example, one KPI is latency, which measures the time it takes to service a request. If you begin seeing latency increase or deviate from an acceptable range, it is probably time to issue an alert and have someone take a look at it. In addition to KPIs, you can use other signals and metrics to determine why something is failing.

Continuous Testing in Production

Using continuous testing you can generate requests that are sent throughout the system and simulate real users. You can utilize this traffic to get test coverage for the components, discover potential issues, and test your monitoring and alerting. Following are some common continuous testing practices:

- Blue/green deployments
- Canary testing
- A/B testing

These practices are discussed in Chapter 5.

Start with Basic Metrics

Ensure that you are always collecting traffic (how much demand is placed on the component), latency (the time it takes to service a request), and errors (rate of requests that fail) for each component in your system.

Service Communication

Service communication is an important part of cloud native applications. Whether it's a client communicating with a backend, a service communicating with a database, or the individual services in a distributed architecture communicating with one another, these interactions are an important part of cloud native applications. Many different forms of communication are used depending on the requirements. The following subsections offer some best practices for service communication.

Design for Backward and Forward Compatibility

With backward compatibility, you ensure that new functionality added to a service or component does not break any existing service. For example, in Figure 6-3, Service A v1.0 works with Service B v1.0. Backward compatibility means that the release of Service B v1.1 will not break the functionality of Service A.

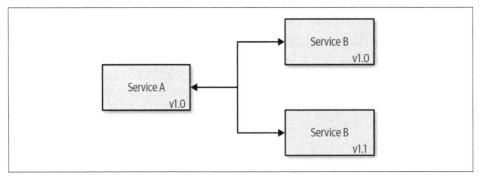

Figure 6-3. Backward compatibility

To ensure backward compatibility, any new fields added to the API should be optional or have sensible defaults. Any existing fields should never be renamed, because that will break the backward compatibility.

Parallel change, also known as the *Expand and Contract* pattern, can be used to safely introduce backward-incompatible changes. As an example, say a service owner would like to change a property or resource on an interface. The service owner will expand the interface with a new property or resource, and then after all consumers have had a chance to move the service interface, the previous property is removed.

If your system or components need to ensure rollback functionality, you will need to think about the forward compatibility as you're making changes to your service. Forward compatibility means that your components are compatible with future versions. Your service should be able to accept "future" data and messaging formats and handle them appropriately. A good example of forward compatibility is HTML: when it encounters an unknown tag or attribute, it's not going to fail; it will just skip it.

Define Service Contracts That Do Not Leak Internal Details

A service that exposes an API should define contracts and test against the contracts when releasing updates. For example, a REST-based service would generally define a contract in the OpenAPI format or as documentation, and consumers of the service would build to this contract. Updates to the service can be pushed, and as long as it doesn't introduce any breaking changes to the API contract, these releases would not affect the consumer. Leaking internal implementations of a service can make it difficult to make changes and introduces coupling. Don't assume a consumer is not using some piece of data exposed through the API.

Services that publish messages to a queue or a stream should also define a contract in the same way. The service publishing the events will generally own the contract.

Prefer Asynchronous Communication

Use asynchronous communication whenever possible. It works well with distributed systems and decouples the execution of two or more services. A message bus or a stream is often used when implementing this approach, but you could use direct calls through something like gRPC as well. Both use a message bus as a channel.

Use Efficient Serialization Techniques

Distributed applications like those built using a microservices architecture rely more heavily on communications and messaging between services. The data serialization and deserialization can add a lot of overhead in service communication.

In one case, serialization and deserialization were found to account for nearly 40% of the CPU utilization across all the services. Replacing the standard JSON serialization library with a custom one reduced this overhead to roughly 15% of overall CPU utilization.

Use efficient serialization formats like protocol buffers, commonly used in gRPC. Understand the trade-offs with the different serialization formats, because tooling and consumer requirements might not make this a feasible option. You can also use other techniques to reduce the need for serialization in some services by placing some of the data into headers. For example, if a service receives a request and operates on only a handful of fields in a large message payload before passing it to a downstream service, by putting these fields into headers the service does not need to deserialize or reserialize the payload. The service reads and writes headers and then simply passes the entire payload through to the downstream services.

Use Queues or Streams to Handle Heavy Loads and Traffic Spikes

A queue or a stream between components acts as a buffer and stores the message until it is retrieved. Using a queue allows the components to process the messages at their own pace, regardless of the incoming volume or load. Consequently, this helps maximize the availability and scalability of your services.

Batch Requests for Efficiency

Queues can be used for batching multiple requests and performing an action only once. For example, it is more efficient to write 1,000 batched entries into the database instead of one entry at a time 1,000 times.

Split Up Large Messages

Sending, receiving, and manipulating large messages requires more resources and can slow down your entire system. The *Claim-Check* pattern talks about splitting a large message into two parts. You store the entire message in an external service (database, for example) and send only the reference to the message. Any interested message receivers can use the reference to obtain the full message from the database.

Containers

It's possible to run most applications in a Docker container without very much effort. However, there are some potential pitfalls when running containers in production and streamlining the build, deployment, and monitoring. A number of best practices have been identified to help avoid the pitfalls and improve the results.

Store Images in a Trusted Registry

Any images running on the platform should come from the trusted container image registry. Kubernetes exposes a webhook (validating admission) that can be used to ensure pods can use images only from a trusted registry. If you're using Google Cloud, you can take advantage of the binary authorization security measure that ensures only trusted images are deployed on your cluster.

Utilize the Docker Build Cache

Using the build cache when building Docker images can speed up the build process. All images are built up from layers, and each line in the Dockerfile contributes a layer to the final image. During the build, Docker will try to reuse a layer from a previous build instead of building it again. However, it can reuse only the cached layers if all previous build steps used it as well. To get the most out of the Docker build cache, put the commands that change more often (e.g., adding the source code to the image, building the source code) at the end of the Dockerfile. That way, any preceding steps will be reused.

Don't Run Containers in Privileged Mode

Running containers in privileged mode allows access to everything on the host. Use the security policy on the pod to prevent containers from running in privileged mode. If a container does for some reason require privileged mode to make changes to the host environment, consider separating that functionality from the container and into the infrastructure provisioning.

Use Explicit Container Image Tags

Always tag your container images with specific tags that tightly link the container image to the code that is packaged in the image. To tag the images properly, you can either use a Git commit hash that uniquely identifies the version of the code (e.g., 1f7a7a472) or use a semantic version (e.g., 1.0.1). The tag latest is used as a default value if no tag is provided; however, because it's not tightly linked to the specific version of the code, you should avoid using it. The latest tag should never be used in a production environment because it can cause inconsistent behavior that can be difficult to troubleshoot.

Keep Container Images Small

In addition to taking up less space in a container registry or the host system using the image to run a container, smaller images improve image push and pull performance. This in turn improves the performance when you start containers as part of deploying or scaling a service. The application and its dependencies will have some impact on the size of the image, but you can reduce most of the image size by using lean base images and ensuring that unnecessary files are not included in the image. For example, the alpine 3.9.4 image is only 3 MB, with the Debian stretch image at 45 MB, and the CentOS 7.6.1810 at 75 MB. The distributions generally offer a slim version that removes more from the base image that might not be needed by the application. Generally, there are two things to keep in mind for keeping images lean:

- Start with a lean base image
- Include only the files needed for the operation of the application

You can use the Container Builder pattern to create lean images by separating the images used to build the artifacts from the base image used to run the application. Docker's multistage build is often used to implement this. You can create Docker build files that can start from different images used for executing the commands to build and test artifacts, and then define another base image as part of creating the image to run the application.

 Using a *.dockerignore* file can improve build speed by excluding files that are not needed in the Docker build.

Run One Application per Container

Always run a single application within a container. Containers were designed to run a single application, with the container having the same life cycle as the application running in the container. Running multiple applications within the same container makes it difficult to manage, and you might end up with a container in which one of the processes has crashed or is unresponsive.

Use Verified Images from Trusted Repositories

There's a large and growing number of publicly available images that are helpful when working with containers. Docker repository tags are mutable, so it's important to understand that the images can change. When using images in an external repository it's best to copy or re-create them from the external repository into one managed by the organization. The organization's repository is usually closer to the CI services, and this approach removes another service dependency that could impact build.

Use Vulnerability Scanning Tools on Images

You need to be aware of any vulnerabilities that affect your images because this can compromise the security of your system. If a vulnerability is discovered, you need to rebuild the image with the patches and fixes included and then redeploy it. Some cloud providers offer vulnerability scanning with their image registry solutions, so make sure you are taking advantage of those features.

 Scan an image as often as possible because new cybersecurity vulnerabilities and exposures (CVE) are released daily.

Don't Store Data in Containers

Containers are ephemeral—they can be stopped, destroyed, or replaced without any loss of data. If the service running in a container needs to store data, use a volume mount to save the data. The contents in a volume exist outside the life cycle of a container and a volume does not increase the size of a container. If the container requires temporary nonpersistent writes, use a tmpfs mount, which will improve performance by avoiding writes to a container's writable layer.

Never Store Secrets or Configuration Inside an Image

Hardcoding any type of secrets within an image is something you want to avoid. If your container requires any secrets, define them within environment variables or as files, mounted to the container through a volume.

Summary

We could easily fill an entire book covering best practices for cloud native applications given the number of technologies involved. However, there are certain areas that have been coming up repeatedly in customer conversations, and this chapter has covered a collection of best practices, tips, and proven patterns for cloud native applications for those areas. You should have a better understanding of the factors you may want to consider.

CHAPTER 7

Portability

Portability is sometimes a concern when building cloud native applications. The application might have a requirement to be deployed across multiple cloud providers or even on-premises. These requirements are generally driven by stakeholders, whether they are customers using the application or the business building the application. It might be the case that the application is deployed by the customer, either on their own hardware or in their own account on the cloud provider of their choice. Regardless of the reasons, the requirement for portability should be treated like any other architecturally significant requirement. It should be driven by the business with careful consideration to the costs and trade-offs.

Why Make Applications Portable?

There are many good reasons to make applications portable. Portability should be a requirement, and the trade-offs and costs associated with the feature should be considered. Following are some of the reasons why software vendors make applications portable:

- Building an application that's deployed into a customer's environment and there's a requirement to offer deployment into the customer's choice of cloud provider or on-premises.

- Building a hybrid application that runs in the cloud and on-premises, where some of the services in the application run in both environments.

- Services need to be near a customer's application in order to minimize latency. These could be services that store or analyze data, for example.

- Some aspect of an application will benefit from a service offered by another cloud provider. A feature of the application would be deployed into another cloud vendor, different from the primary application features.

- Disaster recovery and backup for services requiring extremely high levels of availability.

- Leverage with the cloud provider account management team to negotiate better pricing.

- Agility to move workloads for cost savings or to take advantage of some new functionality in another cloud provider.

Some applications are made to be portable only out of fear of vendor lock-in. Vendor lock-in happens when an application has dependencies on services or APIs that are only available from a specific cloud provider. This can make it difficult to move the application without refactoring and potentially rewriting parts of the application and/or tooling used to manage the application. Some teams will invest a lot of resources making an application portable without considering these costs. It's important to understand the trade-offs when portability is a requirement. Stakeholders will sometimes request that an application is portable without understanding that there are in fact trade-offs potentially affecting time to market, features, engineering costs, and, quite often, increased operational costs.

Sometimes, engineering teams will needlessly make an application portable, even though there is no requirement for it. This often happens out of a fear of making a decision to commit to a cloud provider. What happens if the other cloud providers services become less expensive, a feature is added, or one becomes more popular? This fear of being locked in can even delay a project start date because the team spends time evaluating platforms and techniques.

The Costs of Portability

Application portability generally comes with a price tag, and with larger applications this cost can be significant. Making an application portable—one that can be deployed on multiple cloud providers or on-premises—might be a requirement. If so, it's important to understand the associated costs and potential trade-offs. The business needs to consider these trade-offs so it can prioritize portability against other features, and determine whether it's even worth the additional cost. If, for example, the business is considering portability as a requirement, it would be important to know how this might affect operational costs or time to market. It might be the case that portability is not worth the increased costs.

Here are some potential costs to consider when evaluating portability requirements:

- Increased operational costs as a result of not using vendor-specific managed services

- Increased infrastructure costs as a result of not using cloud provider products and services not available on all cloud providers

- Increased engineering costs as a result of implementing features that might only be available from one of the target cloud providers

- Increased engineering costs as a result of using technologies outside the team's skillset

- Reduced performance as a result of placing layers between services

- Increased testing costs necessary to verify the application's function on supported providers

- Lost revenue as a result of delayed value delivery to customers

 The operational costs need to be carefully considered, as they can increase significantly. Most will only consider portability of compute, but managing dependent services, like queues, streams, data storage, and analytics services, can add a lot of operational burden.

Data Gravity and Portability

Data gravity is a term coined by Dave McCrory. The concept is fairly simple: data wants to be near the applications using it. As the data grows, its gravitational force increases, pulling applications and additional data to it. The larger the data, the more gravitational pull. Every major cloud provider understands the importance of data gravity as well as the challenges inherent in moving the data to another cloud vendor.

Indeed, moving data from one cloud provider to another is often the most challenging aspect of moving an application. Some businesses invest a lot of resources making the application portable without understanding the inherent challenges. The cost of moving the data along with the potential for incurring downtime are often not worth it; thus, the investments in making an application portable are wasted.

Most of the major cloud vendors provide data migration services that can make it easier to move data around, but with large amounts of data, this can still be a large effort. Moving data without taking an application offline can be challenging and expensive. You can use techniques like moving data that is no longer changing before a migration to minimize this downtime. You also can use live replication of the data during the transition.

When and How to Implement Portability

Some or all of an application's portability requirements can be addressed at the start of an application or later in its lifetime. If portability is going to be a future requirement, some things can be done at the start to make it easier to add this requirement. You can use good coding practices that organize the code into separate concerns and layers. You can take advantage of technologies available across cloud providers and that don't involve a significant trade-off. Something as simple as using MongoDB or PostgreSQL can go a long way toward enabling application portability. These data storage technologies are available as managed services and can be deployed on-premises. Also, consider the trade-offs when choosing not to use a vendor's product that might be well integrated with other products. For example, data storage services offered by cloud providers will integrate security or event handling with other services in the platform.

Standardized Interfaces

Standardization can make it easier to build portable applications, but the standardization process can move slowly, often requiring teams across different organizations to agree on the standards. Given the pace at which technology and the cloud moves, this can be a challenge. This is not the case with all standards, and using popular standards should be something to consider when you're building portable applications.

OpenAPI, for example, is a standard that API management products use when defining REST-based gateway services. Developers are able to create an API definition with OpenAPI and use much of it across the various cloud vendor gateways. There can be some vendor-specific settings that will need to be added to the definition, but these can be minimized. The open service broker API is another example of a standard interface that platforms can use to provision and manage cloud vendor resources through a platform like Kubernetes.

Service Mesh Interface (SMI) defines an interface that you can use to provide interoperability across different service mesh technologies like Istio, Consul, and Linkerd. There are a growing number of service mesh technologies available today, without a standard interface, and developers adopting these technologies need to commit to one and implement features directly against the API. Standardized interfaces like SMI enable portability and flexibility, allowing applications to easily and quickly adapt to fast-changing requirements, environments, and a growing ecosystem of technologies.

Many of the "standards" that can be used in an application to address portability are interfaces created and used in popular products that others have adopted. MongoDB is the most popular NoSQL document-oriented database today. Cloud vendors like Microsoft and Amazon have, for example, created databases that look like a MongoDB database by implementing the MongoDB API. Applications that target MongoDB might be able to be moved to one of these databases that look like MongoDB. The entire set of features, however, might not be implemented in these services. This can mean implementing additional functionality in the application because it might not be possible to take full advantage of the features available in MongoDB.

Containers

No section on portability would be complete without covering containers. Containers, a standard packaging format that encapsulates code and dependencies, can make it very easy to move application code. By packaging the application and dependencies into containers, you can use one of the many cloud provider services to run the application in the container. The widespread adoption of the Docker container format has helped to make containers very portable.

Placing an application into a container might not necessarily make it portable. If the application connects to a cloud vendor–specific service, like some logging service, that will need to be changed to run the application on-premises or in another cloud vendor. Consider external dependencies when building applications and use Twelve-Factor application methodologies. For example, one of the Twelve-Factor methodologies is to treat logs as event streams. The application should be not concerned with the routing or storage of this stream. By logging to standard out, the execution environment can be configured to send logs to a location best suited for the environment in which it's running.

Common Services and Features

Using the lowest common set of technologies and features available from the cloud providers can help meet portability requirements. However, doing so can also increase costs or potentially reduce application functionality. For example, an application that requires a relational database might use PostgreSQL instead of Oracle. All of the major cloud vendors offer PostgreSQL and MySQL as fully managed services. Although the engineering team might be more comfortable with a Microsoft SQL Server database, it might be worth training developers and/or bringing in a consultant with the experience to ensure portability without increased operational costs. Many of the more popular open source technologies are available as managed services. For example, Redis, PostgreSQL, MySQL, and Kubernetes are available as managed services on Amazon Web Services (AWS), Google Cloud Platform, and Microsoft Azure.

Abstractions and Layers

A common approach to portability is to use abstractions and layers. These abstractions can be configurable libraries in the application, generic representations that are transformed, or service facades that sit between the application and the cloud provider's services. The cloud provider–specific layers can be replaced using either component substitution techniques in the application code or connecting to services through platform-specific facades. An additional benefit provided by these service abstractions is testing. The providers can be tested independent of the application and can be substituted with mocks to improve local development.

Component substitution

Applications can be built so that their components can be substituted through environment configurations. The providers could be created as libraries and shared across multiple teams. Figure 7-1 depicts how a provider was created for each of the supported data storage services and can be configured based on the environment in which the application is deployed. This approach will increase engineering costs because the components need to be developed and tested. Other challenges often arise when dealing with some feature that's not available in all of the services. This means that the application would then need to use the lowest common denominator and would be unable to take advantage of some feature of the service. Missing features for cloud vendors can be implemented in this layer, or the application can be developed to enable or disable application features when running on different cloud providers.

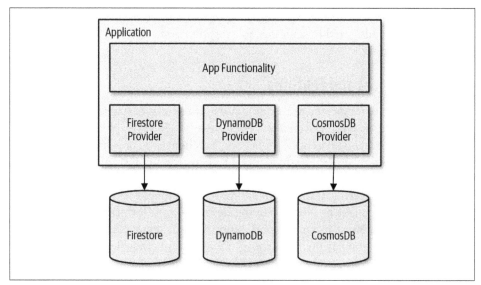

Figure 7-1. Application built with multiple storage providers

Service facade

A service can be placed between the application and the cloud provider services. The application is built against a facade that can be used to interact with the cloud provider services. This basically moves the abstraction out of the process, making it so the application developer does not need to be concerned with these details. Figure 7-2 illustrates how you can deploy the facade as a service with a load balancer to ensure availability, or you can deploy it with the application as a sidecar helper.

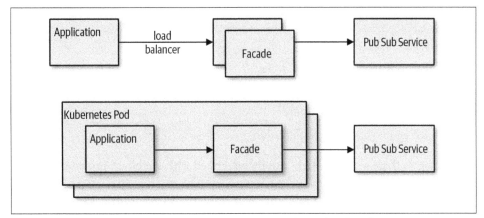

Figure 7-2. Application putting a message on a topic through a facade

There will be increased engineering costs for creating and managing this service. You must also consider that the application developer might not be able to use some potentially useful cloud provider client libraries. This approach will also need to consider how to deal with features that are only available in a single cloud provider. MinIO, discussed later in this chapter, is a good example of a service that not only provides object storage on-premises, but can also be used as a storage adapter.

Transforms

Transforming resources managed in a common format to cloud provider–specific formats is another technique that you can use to target multiple cloud vendors. You can define resources in a generic format and then transform them into cloud provider–specific representations. The serverless framework allows for the definition of serverless configurations in a standard format, which are used to generate cloud vendor–specific configurations.

Managed Services from Other Vendors

Cloud native applications that require portability can also consider using managed services provided by companies independent of the target cloud providers. These services are likewise independent of the cloud provider, and some can even be provisioned in your cloud provider of choice and offer on-premises versions of the services. For example, by using MongoDB as the database in the application, you can use a managed service like MongoDB Atlas when deploying in the cloud. The MongoDB-provided managed service can help eliminate the need to manage the database and reduce operational costs.

Following are some example services:

- Auth0 (*https://auth0.com*)
- MongoDB Atlas (*https://cloud.mongodb.com*)
- Elasticsearch Cloud (*https://www.elastic.co/cloud/*)
- Sendgrid (*https://sendgrid.com*)
- Cloudflare LB (*https://cloudflare.com*)

The billing of these services might not be integrated with the cloud provider's billing, so you'll need to have multiple billing accounts for an application. The other consideration is that these services might not be fully integrated with other services offered by the cloud provider. For example, identity and access services for managing security or triggering a cloud provider function when an event happens might not be possible. These are some things that you will need to consider when you're selecting these types of services.

Portability Tooling

A growing number of portability tools are available, enabling developers to work with cloud services in a provider-agnostic way. These tools create their own layers of abstraction and will use those abstractions to either apply transforms or process the configurations using cloud provider–specific plug-ins. This can make it easy for developers who need to work across multiple cloud providers and possibly make it simplify managing resources that are common across the target cloud providers. There is, however, generally some work for you to do up front understanding the transforms and the provider-specific settings.

Serverless framework

The portability of applications that use Function as a Service (FaaS) is a concern for many software developers with portability requirements because it can be difficult to deal with. Where portability is a requirement, many teams will avoid serverless altogether. This unfortunately means the team cannot take advantage of an extremely powerful set of services. Every cloud provider's serverless products offer a very different set of capabilities that use different configurations and code. For example, the Serverless Framework (*http://serverless.com*) provides an abstraction over popular FaaS technologies. A developer can build to this framework and target any of the platforms supported by the framework. You can extend the framework to support new platforms as well.

When building functions using the Serverless Framework, or even the cloud provider's SDK, it's good practice to separate the event handler from the logic in the function. This makes the code in the function cleaner, easier to test, and much easier to move to another cloud provider if that becomes necessary.

Infrastructure

Each cloud provider exposes a different API for managing the infrastructure. Software developers who need to support multiple cloud provider platforms will generally create abstractions and work against those abstractions for managing cloud infrastructure. Terraform, for example, is a product available from HashiCorp for managing infrastructure across multiple cloud vendors. The tool is useful for supporting an Infrastructure as Code (IaC) approach for managing cloud infrastructure. You can use Terraform to define, change, and version infrastructure in a safe and consistent way. With Terraform, an infrastructure engineer can create a single configuration that can be used to manage multiple cloud providers. In practice, a small percentage of the configuration will be cloud provider specific, although a majority of the configuration can be the same and in a format that's consistent across cloud providers. Figure 7-3 presents an infrastructure engineer creating and maintaining Terraform files and scripts in a source control repository that is capable of targeting multiple cloud vendors. Terraform comes with provisioners for many of the popular cloud providers; the provisioners use the Terraform configurations to provision resources against the cloud provider's specific APIs. The cloud provider–specific provisioner is built to work with the vendor's API and can translate the cloud-agnostic configurations to create and manage resources.

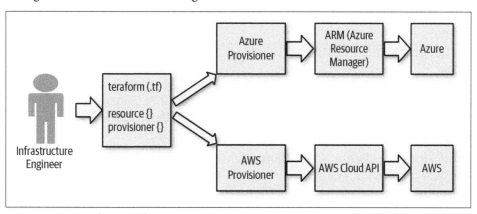

Figure 7-3. Terraform deployment configuration to Azure or AWS

In practice, the Terraform files will likely end up containing some cloud vendor–specific configuration, but you can keep this to a minimum to simplify the management.

Storage abstractions

Applications often need to support different data stores, and patterns like the Repository pattern were often used to accomplish this. You can use a similar approach with cloud applications, but another approach would be to externalize the abstraction from the application through a gateway that can function as the store when on-premises. MinIO is a great example of this. MinIO is an open source object store like the Amazon Simple Storage Service (Amazon S3). The MinIO storage implements the Amazon S3 API, and in addition to storing data on a filesystem volume, you can configure it to work as a gateway. Figure 7-4 depicts an application built to work with data in the MinIO service, which can be configured to act as a gateway to other storage providers. You can even configure the MinIO service to write to the local filesystem when running in a development environment, for example.

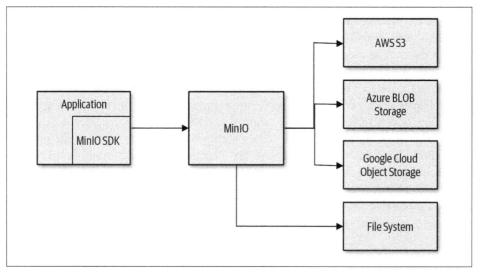

Figure 7-4. MinIO object storage service can be deployed as a gateway

You can deploy the MinIO service as a sidecar container, simplifying the deployment and management of the service. You can deploy multiple instances of the service behind a load balancer in order to make it highly available.

Although the application is more portable, there will be some overhead in the gateway. You will need to evaluate and consider potential performance trade-offs when placing an additional gateway service between the application and storage. The more important thing to consider is that some of the storage features might not be available through the MinIO API, making it necessary to add some vendor-specific implementation that bypasses the MinIO gateway.

Kubernetes as a Portability Layer

You can use Kubernetes to provide an abstraction over the cloud provider infrastructure. You can deploy and manage applications on Kubernetes in a similar manner, regardless of the underlying cloud provider. Kubernetes continues to evolve, providing access to more and more features of the cloud provider's infrastructure through the Kubernetes API.

Every major cloud vendor has a managed Kubernetes service today. The cloud provider–managed Kubernetes service makes it extremely simple to spin up a new Kubernetes cluster. The cloud provider is responsible for the Kubernetes management plane and the cluster is provisioned with the cloud provider–specific plug-ins that are integrated with the underlying infrastructure.

Cloud Controller Manager

Kubernetes has created a pluggable platform enabling cloud provider infrastructure integrations with the platform. This makes it possible to provision cloud provider–specific resources that are used by applications running on Kubernetes, like load balancers and storage volumes, through the Kubernetes interfaces. Figure 7-5 shows the Kubernetes Cloud Controller Manager (CCM) configured with adapters, called *cloud connectors*, that are used to interact with the cloud infrastructure. As a user of a cloud vendor–managed Kubernetes service, it's not likely that you will need to be concerned with these details.

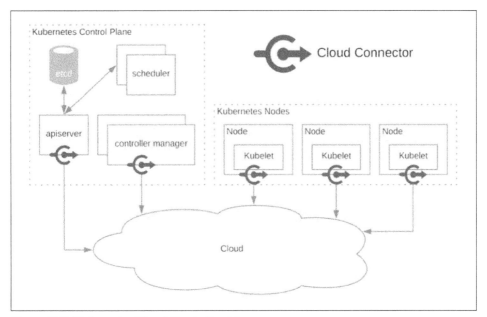

Figure 7-5. Kubernetes Cloud Controller Manager

Service catalog

The Kubernetes service catalog is an extension API that you can use for provisioning managed services from Kubernetes. The service catalog uses the Open Service Broker API to list, provision, and bind to cloud provider–managed services. Figure 7-6 demonstrates how a Kubernetes cluster user can browse through a list of managed services offered through the service broker, provision an instance, and make it available to an application in the cluster. Application developers and operators could, for example, use the Kubernetes API to create a cloud provider–managed PostgreSQL database. Scripts and infrastructure definitions for provisioning application resources would not need to be created for each cloud provider and could simply use Kubernetes regardless of the cloud provider to which the cluster was deployed. This assumes that all of the cloud providers offer a managed PostgreSQL database that is available in the service catalog.

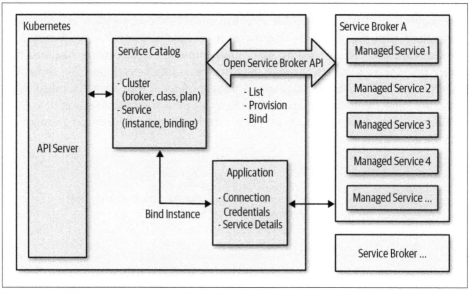

Figure 7-6. Kubernetes service catalog overview

Virtual Kubelet

Virtual Kubelet is an open source project that you can use to make an API look like a *kubelet*, a node in a Kubernetes cluster. This makes it possible to use a cloud vendor's Container as a Service (CaaS) products through Kubernetes. Developers and administrators can continue using the Kubernetes interface to run their workloads and still benefit from the compute services available from the cloud providers. In Figure 7-7 one node in the Kubernetes cluster is virtual, and work scheduled on that node will instead run in another compute service like Azure Container Instances or AWS Fargate. This provides a best-of-breed approach, enabling portability while still providing cloud vendor services without having to build any layers.

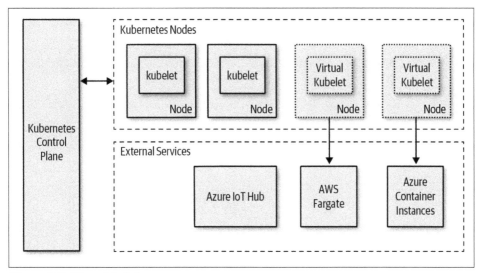

Figure 7-7. Virtual kubelet

Summary

Portability is a feature that a cloud native application must consider. Make sure that you treat it as a requirement and understand the potential trade-offs and costs. In addition to engineering costs, for example, you'll need to consider operational and infrastructure costs. Some planning and good development practices can make it much easier to make an application portable.

Index

Istio, 21
    egress gateway in, 58
    Envoy proxy, 61
    security features, components involved in, 65
    traffic mirroring, 135

J

Jaeger distributed tracing tool, 146
Jepsen tests, 115
JSON, 48
    in document databases, 77
    improving serialization/deserialization, 48
    serialization library, 178

K

k8s (see Kubernetes)
Kata containers, 12
    container runtime interface, 16
key performance indicators (KPIs), 175
key/value stores, 76
knot, 42
Ksync, 125
kube-apiserver, 13
kube-controller-manager, 14
kube-proxy, 14
kube-scheduler, 14
kubelet, 14
Kubernetes
    and containers, 16-17
    as portability layer, 193
        Cloud Controller Manager, 193
        service catalog, 194
        Virtual Kubelet, 194
    building microservices on top of, 21
    ConfigMaps, 149-152
    creating service and deployment for application and Prometheus, 142
    databases on, 103-106
        DaemonSets, 106
        StatefulSets, 105
        storage volumes, 104
    deploying into, using Skaffold development workflow, 128
    development tools for local environment, 124
    development tools for remote environments, 125

Helm tool, using for deployment configuration, 153
Horizontal Pod Autoscaler (HPA), 170
internal and external service communications, 45
isolating pods, 167
local development with remote cluster, 127
overview, 13
probes, 165
role-based access control, 167
Secrets, 152, 166
sidecar proxies, 60
using as deployment platform, deploy stage in CD, 135
using namespaces to organize services, 173
virtual nodes and, 21

L

latency, 138, 176
    in distributed systems, 2
    reducing for data retrieval, 96-100
    response latency in synchronous communication, 54
layers, 187
lean principles and processes, 110
Linkerd, 21
    proxy, 61
Linux
    containers, 9
    containers, running with Amazon Firecracker, 12
liveness, monitoring for services, 148
load balancers
    in cloud native applications, 36
    in stateful, traditional applications, 34
load tests, 115
loading data, 89
    (see also extract, transform, and load)
local development environments, 123, 126
    connection with cloud environment, 123
    container-based, 125
    remote cluster routed to, 129
    tools for running Kubernetes in, 124
    with remote cluster, 127
logging
    in microservice architectures, 27
    including context with log entries, 174
    logs, treating as event streams, 6

reliability
  designing for, in cloud native applications,
    33
  network, fallacy of in distributed systems, 2
ReplicaSets, 15
repositories
  mono-repo vs. poly-repo for source code,
    132
  repository patterns, 192
  verified images from trusted repositories,
    180
request headers in service mesh traffic management,
  ment, 64
request ID headers, 68
request/response, 49
  choosing between pub/sub and, 53
  incoming request rate, 138
  rate limiting and throttling for requests, 165
resiliency
  ensuring, 163-165
    defining CPU and memory limits for
      containers, 165
    graceful degradation, 164
    handling transient failures with retries,
      163
    implementing health checks and readiness
      ness checks, 165
    implementing rate limiting and throttling,
      tling, 165
    using bulkhead pattern, 164
    using circuit breakers for nontransient
      failures, 164
    using finite number of retries, 164
resource versioning, 43
resources
  exhaustion of, in synchronous communications,
    tions, 54
  improved usage with microservices, 25
  limiting consumption of CPU and memory,
    165
  transforming into cloud provider-specific
    formats, 189
REST APIs
  service contracts, defining, 177
  versioning, 43
retries
  handling transient failures with, 163
  in service meshes, 64
  using finite number of, 164

role-based access control (RBAC), 32, 167
rollback functionality, APIs, 45
rollbacks, 177
routing
  AMQP protocol, 48
  by gateways, 55

S

sandboxed containers, 11
scalability, 1
  and cost in cloud native design, 34
  dynamic scaling in and out in cloud native
    architectures, 36
  fast, scalable data, 96-100
  in combined functions and services, 41
  performance and, 169
    designing stateless services that scale out,
      170
    using caching, 170
    using partitioning to scale beyond service
      vice limits, 170
    using platform autoscaling, 170
scaling
  application components having different
    scale requirements, 159
  functions as a service, 42
  improved scale with microservices, 25
  using data partitioning and replication for
    scale, 168
schema on read databases, 77
schema on write databases, 77
schema-first approach (GraphQL), 95
schemas, implementing translations of, 160
search databases, 79
secrets
  never storing in container images, 181
  storing, 152
  storing securely, 166
security
  considerations in cloud native applications,
    31
  database services, 94
  ensuring, 165-167
    encrypting data in transit, 167
    granting least-privileged access, 166
    incorporating security into designs, 166
    isolating Kubernetes pods, 167
    obfuscating data, 166
    securely storing secrets, 166

usability tests, 116, 118, 119
utilization, 138

V

valet key, 93
versioning
    cloud native APIs, 42-45
        compatible versioning, 44
        semantic versioning, 45
    in microservice architectures, 26
Virtual Kubelet, 21, 194
virtual machines (VMs)
    Amazon Firecracker, 12
    containers vs., on a single host, 11
    downsides of using as basis of cloud native
        applications, 11

    from VMs to cloud native, 19-22
        application modernization, 20
        application optimization, 22
        lift and shift, 19
virtual nodes, 21
VirtualService, 122
VM Worker Process, 12
vulnerability scanning tools, using on container
    images, 180

W

WebSockets, 46
    use of MQTT and AMQP messaging proto-
        cols, 48
working with data (see data, working with)

About the Authors

Boris Scholl is a lead product architect with the Azure Compute engineering team focusing on the next generation of distributed systems platforms and application models. He has been working on Azure Developer tools and platforms in various product engineering roles since late 2011. Boris re-joined the Azure Compute team in 2018, after having spent the 18 months outside Microsoft leading an engineering team to work on a microservices platform based on Kubernetes and service meshes. His work on distributed systems platforms has resulted in several patents about cloud computing and distributed systems. Boris is a frequent speaker at industry events, a contributor to many blogs, instructor for distributed computing topics, and the lead author of one of the first books about microservices and Docker on Azure, *Microservices with Docker on Azure* (O'Reilly 2016).

Trent Swanson is a software architect focused on cloud and edge technologies. As a Distinguished Fellow of Cloud Technologies at Johnson Controls, he works with a wide range of cloud technologies and a lot of very smart and passionate people to create intelligent buildings. He has helped teams build and operate large and small applications across multiple cloud providers using modern practices and technologies. As a cofounder and consultant with Full Scale 180, he worked with some of Microsoft's largest customers, helping them migrate and build applications in the cloud. He has been involved in architecting, building, and operating very large-scale applications, utilizing Docker, serverless technologies, and a microservices architecture. He enjoys building and working in high-performing teams who have a learning culture and are capable of quickly applying emerging technologies and processes to support the business.

Peter Jausovec is a software engineer with more than ten years of experience in the field of software development and tech. During his career, he spent time in various roles, starting with QA before moving to software engineering and leading tech teams. His early career was mostly focused on developer and cloud tooling. In recent years, however, he has been focused on developing distributed systems cloud native solutions.

Colophon

The animal on the cover of *Cloud Native* is a purple sandpiper (*Calidris maritima*), a plump shorebird with a large range across arctic and subarctic tundra habitats in North America and Europe. They winter along the rocky coasts of the Atlantic and have the northernmost winter range of any shorebird.

Adults are mostly gray with a slight purplish gloss. They have short, yellow legs and a medium-sized, slightly downcurved bill. On average, they are 9 inches long and weigh 2.5 ounces. Males and females are similar in appearance.

The male purple sandpiper shares responsibility for incubation and then assumes parental care of the hatchlings, which is unusual among monogamous shorebirds. The precocious hatchlings are capable of walking and pecking at the ground for food within a few hours of hatching. Purple sandpipers eat mostly insects, mollusks, spiders, and seeds.

A common behavior of the purple sandpiper and other wading birds is the rodent run, which is a distraction display used to protect the nest from predators. The bird ruffles its feathers, crouches, and runs away from the predator while making a squealing noise that sounds like a mouse. The action resembles the flight response of a small rodent and lures the predator away from the nest.

Many of the animals on O'Reilly covers are endangered; all of them are important to the world.

The cover illustration is by Karen Montgomery, based on a black and white engraving from *British Birds*. The cover fonts are Gilroy Semibold and Guardian Sans. The text font is Adobe Minion Pro; the heading font is Adobe Myriad Condensed; and the code font is Dalton Maag's Ubuntu Mono.